Pushing the Envelope

Pushing the Envelope

CRAFTY PACKAGING
FOR CARDS OF ALL KINDS

LARK BOOKS

A Division of Sterling Publishing Co., Inc.
New York / London

Editor: **Larry Shea**

Art Director: **Celia Naranjo**

Art Production: **Kay Stafford**

Assistant Editors: **Mark Bloom**
Gavin Young

Photography Director: **Dana Irwin**

Photographer: **Stewart O'Shields**

Illustrator: **Orrin Lundgren**

Library of Congress Cataloging-in-Publication Data

Le Van, Marthe.
  Pushing the envelope : crafty packaging for cards of all kinds /
Marthe Le Van. -- 1st ed.
      p. cm.
  Includes index.
  ISBN 978-1-60059-398-7 (trade pbk. : alk. paper)
 1. Greeting cards. 2. Envelopes (Stationery) I. Title.
  TT872.L385 2009
  745.594'1--dc22

                                        2009003810

10 9 8 7 6 5 4 3 2 1

First Edition

Published by Lark Books, A Division of Sterling Publishing Co., Inc.
387 Park Avenue South, New York, NY 10016

© 2009, Lark Books, a Division of Sterling Publishing Co., Inc.

Distributed in Canada by Sterling Publishing,
c/o Canadian Manda Group, 165 Dufferin Street
Toronto, Ontario, Canada M6K 3H6

Distributed in the United Kingdom by GMC Distribution Services,
Castle Place, 166 High Street, Lewes, East Sussex, England BN7 1XU

Distributed in Australia by Capricorn Link (Australia) Pty Ltd.,
P.O. Box 704, Windsor, NSW 2756 Australia

If you have questions or comments about this book, please contact:
Lark Books
67 Broadway
Asheville, NC 28801
828-253-0467

Manufactured in China

ISBN 13: 978-1-60059-398-7

For information about custom editions, special sales, premium and
corporate purchases, please contact Sterling Special Sales Department at
800-805-5489 or specialsales@sterlingpub.com.

contents

The Envelope, please...

❖ If you love crafts that are quick and easy, you're ready to push the envelope.

❖ If you want to make a great impression, you're ready to push the envelope.

❖ If you're living the green life, you're ready to push the envelope.

❖ If you mail cards or give gifts, you're ready to push the envelope.

❖ If you see craft materials everywhere you look—a printed placemat, a stack of junk mail—you're ready to push the envelope.

❖ Because presentation does matter, you're ready to push the envelope.

The creative potential of the envelope has been woefully overlooked. It's been viewed as a purely utilitarian object, ripped open as quickly as possible and discarded just as fast. What's inside an envelope has gotten all the attention. That is, until now!

It's time to push the envelope… literally! To innovate. To go beyond commonly accepted boundaries. Designing and making one-of-a-kind envelopes is a win-win-win crafting opportunity. This book features a veritable smorgasbord of envelope projects with instructions. You can duplicate the fantastic designs step-by-step or let them inspire your own creative path.

The simplest projects, featured in the chapter titled "Ready-made Revamp," start with

commercial envelopes. Embellishing these plain surfaces takes only a matter of minutes, and the results are amazing! Our crafty team of designers also saw a lot of potential in unusual and recycled materials, such as brown paper bags, contact paper, gift wrapping, encyclopedia pages—even coffee filters, an old sweater, and copper mesh. The envelopes they fashioned from these quirky supplies are included in the second project group, "Surprising Supplies." Next, under the banner "Hold Everything," you'll find envelopes that accommodate nontraditional enclosures, such as business cards, CDs, gift cards, and photos. There's even an adorable set of nesting envelopes. Last, but by no means least, "Ready, Set, Fold!" spotlights easy origami envelopes, from a super secret postcard disguise to cheery cherry hearts to a school of funky fish.

There's no need to run out and buy a whole bunch of supplies in order to start making envelopes. You're likely to have almost everything you need already on hand. (Is that good news, or what?) And you probably learned all the necessary skills—like

cutting, folding, and gluing— very early on in life. (It just keeps getting better, doesn't it?) So, with very little expense and very little experience, you can craft imaginative envelopes and have a darn good time doing it. What are you waiting for? The time is now, and you are so ready. Get out there and push the envelope!

the Basics

THE GREATEST THING ABOUT MAKING ENVELOPES is that it's an endeavor with very few rules. You can follow the exact project instructions, or you can make the envelopes as big or small as you wish, embellished to the max, or as clean and simple as you like. Just a few basic tools of the trade will prepare you for hours of envelope entertainment. In no time, you'll be outdoing even the finest store-bought designs.

WILD ABOUT PAPER

Just take a jaunt around the house or head into your home office, and you'll probably find a decent selection of papers. Then familiarize yourself with a few common types that appear in many of the book's projects.

Copier Paper

You might not use this pedestrian paper in the actual envelope design, but good old-fashioned copier paper is valuable to have on hand for sketching ideas, tracing templates, and for practicing folds. You can mess up on the cheap stuff and not feel bad about it!

Card Stock

When you're planning your envelope design, consider the weight of the paper. If you're going to glue a lot of layers on the front of the card or add embellishments, you'll need a heavier-weight card stock or cover-weight paper. Since you'll likely be folding it, make sure it's thin enough to fold but heavy enough to hold your added materials. For many envelopes, a good quality cover-weight card stock works fine. You can explore a variety of card stock colors at craft, art supply, scrapbooking, stamping, or stationery stores. Card stock is sold flat or already folded into an envelope.

Vellum

Paper vellum is a tough, translucent material that comes in a variety of colors, patterns, and finishes. This popular paper is often used to veil images and create an intriguing layered effect. Laser-compatible vellum allows you to print on the paper, which can be a great overlay or elegant enclosure.

Watercolor Paper

If you plan to do any lettering, drawing, or watercoloring on your envelope, it's important to use paper made for those purposes. Acid-free, well-sized paper with a high rag content is the best to use. It's made with cotton fibers rather than wood pulp and usually looks textured or slightly rough.

Commercial Envelopes

If you're in the mood to decorate an envelope but aren't crazy about making one from scratch, no worries! When you buy blank folded cards, they usually come with nice matching envelopes. You can alter them to your heart's content! They come in every imaginable size, color, and shape. Some even have interesting fasteners instead of a traditional flap. You can also find alternative envelopes made from fabric, hemp, and other materials—these are great for dimensional pieces that you would hand deliver rather than mail.

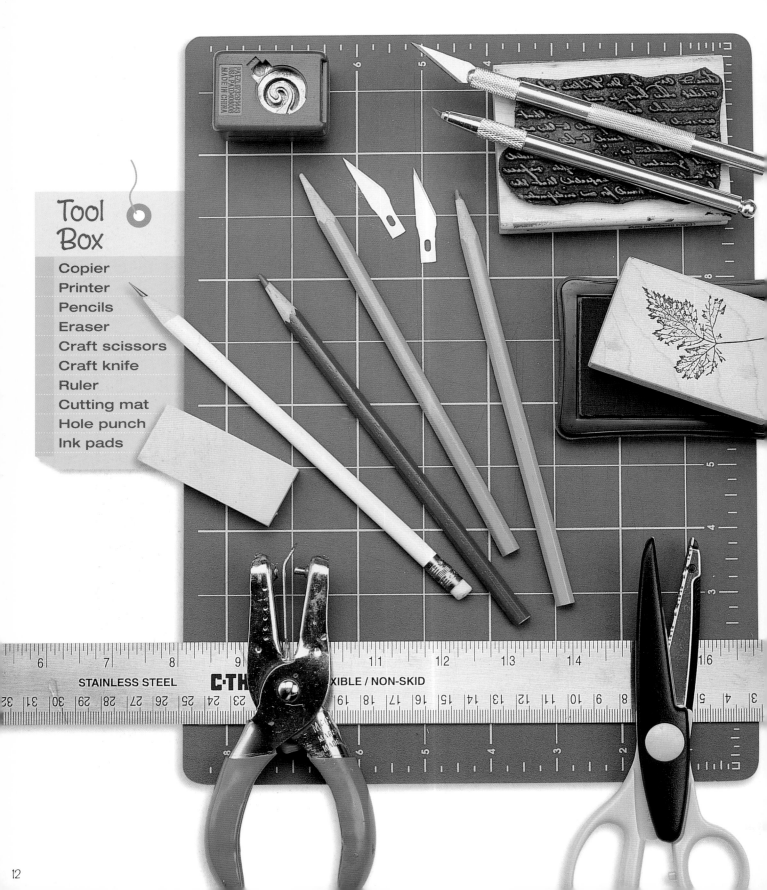

Tool Box

- Copier
- Printer
- Pencils
- Eraser
- Craft scissors
- Craft knife
- Ruler
- Cutting mat
- Hole punch
- Ink pads

TOOL TALK

Most of the tools you need to complete the projects in this book are simple and common. Even the more specialized tools are ones you're probably familiar with. In the list of materials and tools for each project, we've included a reference to the "Tool Box" on page 12 as you'll usually need at least a couple of these items to complete the projects.

Stamps

You can find stamp representations of just about anything, from alphabet letters to zebras. For decorating a series of envelopes, stamps are nice because you can replicate designs without much effort. Consider mixing inks and making your own stamps with potatoes (you'll see how to do just that on page 22).

Bone Folder

With its rounded edges, a bone folder will rake across your fold line giving you a very crisp crease. Other tools can do the trick, too, but a bone folder is ideal for burnishing any spot you've adhered to another, and its blunt point is perfect for scoring paper. When you're going to work with paper, get a bone folder!

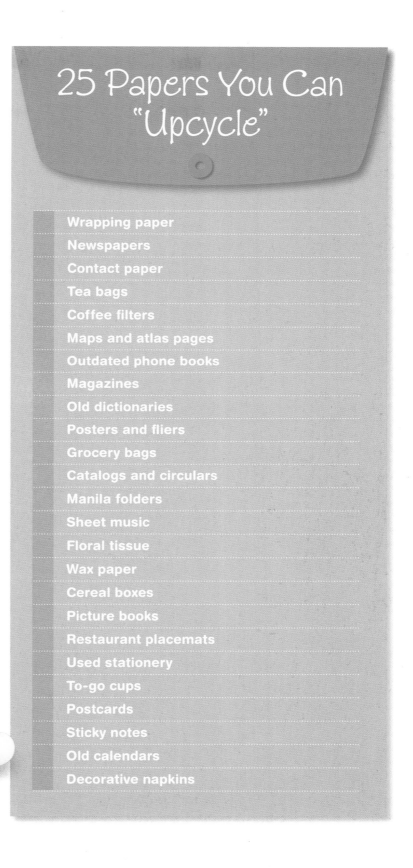

25 Papers You Can "Upcycle"

- Wrapping paper
- Newspapers
- Contact paper
- Tea bags
- Coffee filters
- Maps and atlas pages
- Outdated phone books
- Magazines
- Old dictionaries
- Posters and fliers
- Grocery bags
- Catalogs and circulars
- Manila folders
- Sheet music
- Floral tissue
- Wax paper
- Cereal boxes
- Picture books
- Restaurant placemats
- Used stationery
- To-go cups
- Postcards
- Sticky notes
- Old calendars
- Decorative napkins

ALL THE TRIMMINGS

Adding embellishments to your envelopes takes you beyond necessity and into the wild realm of décor. With any of these little adornments, you can reflect your own individual style and tailor the design to your recipient. Maybe she has a thing for beads—add more. Perhaps you share a love of flowers—include your favorites. Many of the projects you'll encounter use one or more of the embellishments listed here.

Embellishments

Beads
Bows
Brads
Buttons
Charms
Colored staples
Crystals
Decals
Dried and silk flowers
Embroidery floss
Eyelets
Felt
Fleece
Game pieces
Glitter
Grommets
Organza
Pearls
Photos
Pom-poms
Postage stamps
Pressed leaves
Raffia
Rhinestones
Ribbon
Rickrack
Rub-ons
Rubber stamps
Sequins
Stickers
Studs
Tags
Thread
Tulle
Yarn

STICK WITH IT

Depending on the material, method of construction, and intended purpose of your envelopes, some adhesives may work a lot better than others. Luckily, you've got a wide range to choose from.

Glues

Glue sticks are great because they easily glide across the surface of whatever you're gluing, leaving a smooth, even film. Cleanup involves no more than putting the cap back on. Keep in mind that the drying time is really fast, so be sure you're satisfied with the work you are pasting in place.

Tacky craft glue is suitable for embellishing your envelopes with objects such as beads or charms. It's thicker than common white craft glue—polyvinyl acetate or PVA—and it dries clear.

Hot glue with a glue gun is a handy and strong adhesive, but it also can be used to create an easy dimensional effect. First, use the hot glue to draw designs on your envelope, and then after the glue dries, simply paint over it.

Multipurpose spray adhesive has the advantage of drying quickly, but you'll need to know exactly where you want to place your material before using it.

Work in a well-ventilated room and keep scrap paper beneath your project to protect your surface from a sticky mess.

Tapes

Masking tape is useful to stick things together as long as the tape is hidden. The exception to the rule is when masking tape is used as part of your design, as in the project Modern Art on page 28.

Cellophane tape is clear and affixes to a surface with very little pressure. It's not the best choice if you need a sturdy hold, but it's fine when you need just a little adhesion.

Double-sided tape comes in handy as a sealing device for envelope flaps, and sometimes it can replace glue altogether.

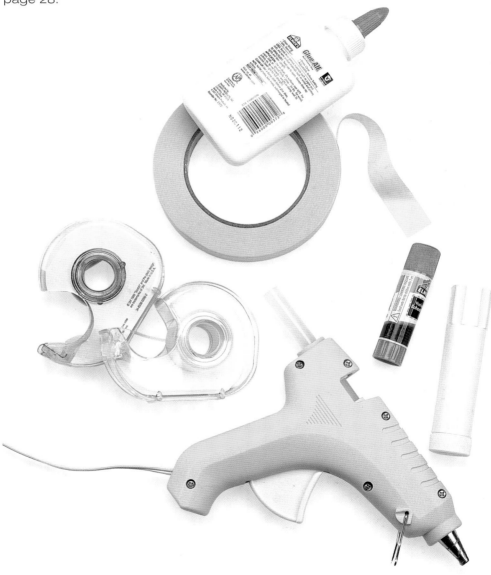

ALL SEWN UP

To complete some of the projects in this book, you may need to do some stitching. Depending on your skill or preference, you can sew by hand or by machine.

Hand Sewing Techniques

Hand sewing is perfect for projects involving delicate paper, metallic or heavy-fiber threads, or specific embroidery stitches you can't get from a machine.

Needles

Your choice of needle depends on your choice of paper and thread. Use a slender, sharp needle for delicate paper and a large-eyed needle with a blunter tip for heavier paper. A general sewing needle is satisfactory for most projects.

Threads

What an easy way to change up a project. Use different types of threads to suit your taste. Rayon, cotton, linen, and polyester sewing threads work well with paper and other materials.

Embroidery floss is popular for hand-sewn projects and comes in about a million colors. Each skein of floss is made up of six strands. For a delicate design, use two or three strands, or use all six for more heft.

Twine is a strong thread or string made from two or fewer strands of yarns twisted together. You can find twine in a variety of natural fibers, such as cotton, sisal, hemp, and jute. Use this when you really need to hold it together.

Stitches

When hand sewing on paper, it's best to use a longer stitch length and keep the lines of your stitches spaced well apart from each other. Don't knot the thread as you would when sewing on fabric, but use an adhesive like glue or tape instead. The following common stitches can come in handy when you're sewing by hand.

Straight Line Stitch

Also called a running stitch, this is the simplest stitch, used for creating straight lines of any length. Simply take your needle through the wrong side to the right side of your work and stitch, making a stitch to the desired length, and then bring the needle back through.

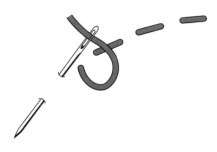

Blanket Stitch

Working from left to right, bring the needle to the right side of the fabric/paper on the edge. Make an upright stitch to the right with the needle pointed down. Catch the thread under the point of the needle as you come out of the edge.

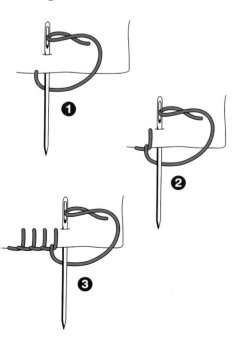

Machine Sewing Techniques

Machine sewing on paper is much the same as sewing on fabric, and you can accomplish it with just about any sewing machine. It's faster than hand sewing and might be a good option for large projects.

High-end sewing machines offer a wide variety of decorative stitches, but even the simplest machines offer a few alternatives so you can achieve interesting effects, such as a zigzag or featherstitch. Use tightly spaced zigzag stitches to emulate embroidery stitches and reinforce buttonholes.

Tips:
Machine Sewing on Paper
- Use a small needle.
- Keep the machine speed slow.
- Keep a loose stitch density.
- Use the longest stitch possible.
- Have enough thread in the bobbin to finish the job.
- Keep some extra needles on hand.
- Don't stitch more than three layers of paper at a time.
- Do a test run!

Stick It Without Licking It

Tired of the dreaded "envelope-glue tongue?" Or just want to try something different? Here are a dozen ways to close an envelope without glue:

- Paint on a thin layer of clear nail polish
- Stick on a sticker
- Seal it with wax
- Staple it shut
- Button it up
- Snap it together
- Apply colorful or unusual tape
- Cut a tab
- Add a pop rivet
- Apply adhesive bandages (perfect for get-well cards!)
- Re-use fruit and vegetable stickers
- Place the return address label across the flap
- Use a piece of chewing gum (the ultimate in recycling)

ENVELOPE ANATOMY

Envelopes are simple, right? True, but there are still some terms to become familiar with if you want to know which end is up. These illustrations show the various parts of an envelope. Variations on these parts are what create different envelope styles.

Flap Styles

Pointed

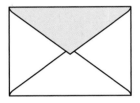

Commercial

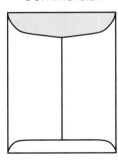

Wallet

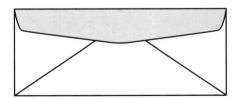

Square

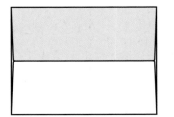

Envelope Parts

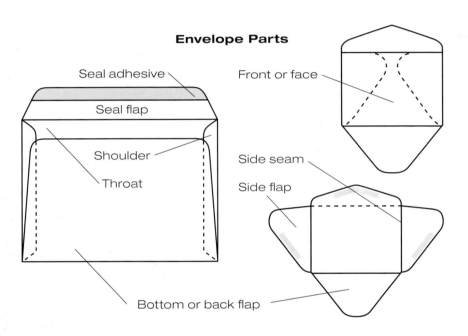

Seal adhesive

Seal flap

Shoulder

Throat

Front or face

Side seam

Side flap

Bottom or back flap

Opening Styles

Open side

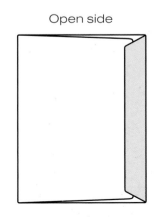

Open end

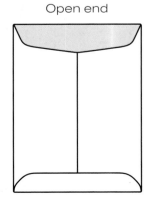

Cutting, Folding & Scoring

While some of the envelope projects don't involve paper at all, it's a good idea to know some simple rules about cutting, scoring, and folding for those that do. Before you make that first cut, determine the size of your envelope. If in doubt, use a piece of scrap paper to make a prototype of the envelope, and then, when satisfied, use it as a pattern for cutting. Always make sure your cuts are neat and clean, regardless of the tool you use (for example, scissors or craft knife).

Do yourself a favor and score the paper before folding it. Scoring breaks the top fibers in the paper to ensure an even fold exactly where you want it. To score the paper, first use a ruler andpencil to lightly mark your fold line on the inside of the paper you plan to fold. Then hold the ruler against that line while running the sharp point of a bone folder along the edge of the ruler. Fold the paper along the scored line. Use the curved side of the bone folder to press the paper flat at the fold, and you're all set!

Going Beyond Paper

Just because most envelopes are made of paper, yours don't have to be. There's a whole wide world of foldable, recyclable materials out there for you to explore.

Plastics

- Bread wrappers
- Shopping bags
- Newspaper and magazine wrappers
- Bubble wrap (who doesn't love that popping sound?)
- Trash bags
- To-go containers (wash them first!)

Fibers

- Pillowcases and sheets
- Washcloths and dishrags
- T-shirts
- Baby clothes (they grow so fast!)
- Polishing cloths
- Socks (where'd the other one go?)
- Pantyhose with runs
- Hole-y jeans

Other Broken & Recycled Items

- Umbrellas
- Beach balls
- Lawn chairs (love that webbing!)

ORIGAMI WITHOUT TEARS

Origami is the ancient Japanese art of paper folding. The term comes from—and this makes a lot of sense—the words *oru* ("folding") and *kami* ("paper"). The traditional goal of this art is to start with only one piece of paper and—without using any glue or cuts—to create a representation of an object using geometric folds and crease patterns.

The art of origami only uses a small number of different folds, but they can be combined to make an endless array of intricate creations. The most familiar form is probably the Japanese paper crane. These designs usually begin with a square sheet of paper whose sides may be different colors or prints.

The origami projects in this book are not very complicated, and you fold them with a variety of papers: transparent paper, newspaper, gift wrap, writing paper, and even restaurant placemats. You can decorate the paper before or after you fold it. And here's an idea: Instead of using the final product to hold an enclosed letter, consider writing your letter on the paper being folded, so the recipient unfolds your message as they open the envelope!

You'll notice that our origami envelope projects require helping folds. To accomplish a helping fold, you fold over the paper in the direction given, then fold it back to leave a crease that will help guide you later in the project.

Tip

Grab your ruler or bone folder. It helps to keep the edges of the fold straight if you place a flat ruler along the fold line and fold up the edge over the ruler.

Envelope Worthy

Maybe that faceless bank you mail your credit-card bill to won't be impressed with your handmade envelopes. (Though if your payment is a few days late, it might be worth a shot.) There are still many, many other things that could find a perfect home in just the right envelope. Here are just a few.

Love notes

Ticket stubs

Lipsticak kisses

IOUs

Gift cards

Cash

The rent

Plane tickets

CDs

Photos

Business cards

Predictions

Sizes for loved one (don't forget your ring size!)

Perfume on a piece of paper

Cherished recipes

Extra keys

Resolutions

Passwords

Quotes and sayings for tough times

Three wishes

Things you can't say out loud

Poems and song lyrics

Lists of your favorite things

readymade
revamps

chapter 1

Rethink, remodel, and redecorate store-bought envelopes into super works of art

you say potato

Lila Ruby King

Finished Size
6³⁄₈ x 4½ inches
(16.2 x 11.4 cm)

Variation
Try making your own envelope. Print it while it is a flat sheet, before folding, so you get an allover pattern.

what you do

1. Cut each potato in half on the chopping board. For larger potatoes, try cutting a thick slice. Put the potatoes, cut side down, onto paper towels to let them dry out a little.

2. Draw your design onto the potato surface using a marker or pen. Remember that you won't be able to get a high level of detail with a potato; simple shapes will work best.

3. Using the woodcutting tools and/or the craft knife, cut around your design. You want to cut down far enough that the ink won't touch the areas of the potato that you don't want, so about ¼ inch (6 mm) to ½ inch (1.3 cm) is perfect. You

may need to dab the potato on the paper towel again to get rid of any extra moisture.

4. Now press the cut design into your ink pad. You can use the special ink pads for stamping, or even just the sort you find in the office. You can even apply a layer of paint instead of ink. Once the potato is inked, you can do some test stampings. This way you can see if there are any areas of the stamp that you need to cut back further. This is also a good way to get the hang of how much pressure you need to apply to get the perfect print.

5. Once you are happy with your stamp, ink up and stamp your envelope. You can even use

the stamp to make matching cards and wrapping paper.

6. When you have finished stamping, lay the prints flat on a bench or table to dry.

Note: A potato stamp will last only a day or two at the most, so make sure you get all the prints you need while you still have it!

Variation: After you have mastered the potato stamp, try carving other materials. A simple eraser works really well, and you can find carving blocks specially made for block printing in an arts supply store or catalog. These blocks are very easy to carve into, and you can achieve a higher level of detail in the design.

butterfly kisses

Sharon Rohloff

24

what you need

Tool Box (page 12)

Business-size envelope

Acrylic stamps of a butterfly, trellis, and mailing label

Pigment ink in lime green, lilac, orange, and metallic gold

Watermark ink

Embossing powder in complementary colors

Heat gun

Copier paper or stationery

Finished Size

Envelope: 9½ x 4 inches
(24.1 x 10.2 cm)

Paper: 8½ x 11 inches
(21.6 x 27.9 cm)

what you do

1. Stamp a mailing label shape on the right side of the envelope in pigment ink in the color of your choice.

2. Pounce the same color of ink halfway across the envelope, with deeper color on the left fading to no color on the right.

3. Use a large acrylic stamp and the same color of ink to create the trellis on the upper left-hand corner. To achieve a burnished effect, stamp again lightly with gold metallic ink directly over the image.

4. Use a small flower stamp to add flowers to your trellis and the mailing label edge.

5. Stamp a butterfly to the left of the label with watermark ink. Add embossing powder in a matching color and heat to emboss.

6. Repeat steps 2–5 to create the stationery, pouncing extra ink in the lower right-hand corner of your page to balance your design.

Variation
Use lilac and metallic silver ink for an elegant look suitable for anniversary or bridal shower invitations.

Joan K. Morris

knockout punch

Play peek-a-boo with printed stationery sets

Finished Size
5¾ x 4½ inches
(14.6 x 11.4 cm)

what you do

1. Look through the underside of the ¾-inch (1.9 cm) hole punch, and choose an area of one of the printed cards to punch out.

2. To make rings, first punch out the 1-inch (2.5 cm) hole. Look from the underside of the 1½-inch (3.8 cm) hole punch, center the first hole, and punch out the ring. Don't worry about making a mistake, because if the ring is off center it looks great too.

3. Make an assortment of round pieces and rings. Cut out some shapes with the scissors, too, and lay them all out in front of you.

4. Play around with punching holes out of the envelope flap or the body in the back or even all the way through the envelope. Just be sure you leave room for the address and return address on the front of the envelope. Also, try to punch any hole where it will show the design on the card the best. Your only limitation is how far the hole punch can go in on the envelope.

5. Glue the cutouts onto the envelopes with the glue stick. Position the rings around the holes you punched in the envelopes or around the circles you punched out. You can also glue part of a circle onto the edge of the flap and let it hang over the flap.

modern
art

Heather
Crossley

28

what you need

Tool Box (page 12)

Masking tape

Nonstick surface

Acrylic paints

Paintbrush

Plain commercial envelopes

what you do

1. Place strips of masking tape side by side on a surface where they can be easily removed without losing their stickiness. Also make sure the surface is one that you can paint on and discard (or clean up later). The back of a cutting mat, a plastic tray, an acrylic or glass surface, or the cover or back of a rectangular plastic container work well.

2. Randomly paint the masking tape with a variety of paints. Add highlights with metallic or dimensional paints if you like.

3. Allow the tape to thoroughly dry.

4. When the tape is dry, remove and stick it down directly onto your plain commercial envelopes. You can stick it down by panels, slice up the tape into patterned strips, or randomly tear pieces, as in the examples shown.

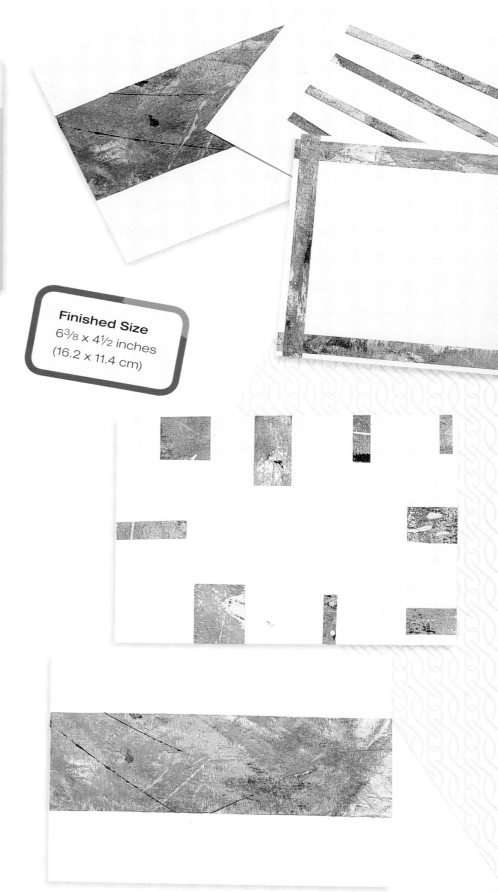

Finished Size
6³⁄₈ x 4¹⁄₂ inches
(16.2 x 11.4 cm)

collection
of curiosities

COME INTO MY PARLOR

CATS

BODY AND SOUL

HAND

DELIVER

Mar Goman

what you need

Tool Box (page 12)

Old book pages or other found papers

Distress ink, thinned paint, or even an ink pad

Paper towels

Commercial envelopes (or make your own)

Glue stick

Toner-based copies of small images

Colorless blender transfer pen

Transparent tape

Colored pencils or watercolors (optional)

Rubber stamps (optional)

Finished Size
8⅞ x 4½ inches
(22.5 x 11.4 cm)

what you do

1. Select some found papers, such as old dictionary pages. If you wish to stain your papers, use distress ink or some thinned acrylic paint. Scrunch up a paper towel and dip it in a bit of the ink, or even on a pre-inked stamp pad, and lightly rub over your paper to give it an irregular, aged look.

Tip
Postage stamps that match the transferred images add a clever touch. Visit local stamp shows or stores that cater to stamp collectors to find some.

2. When the found paper is dry, tear or cut it to fit the envelope. Glue it down securely with the glue stick. Smooth it carefully and completely.

3. Select the images you want to use and copy them on a toner-based copier, like the ones found in most commercial copy stores. If your image has any text, ask someone at the copy store how to use the "reverse" feature. This will make the text read correctly on your envelope.

4. Once you have your copies, the easiest way to transfer them is to use a colorless blender pen. You will want to practice this transfer technique on scrap paper before doing it on your envelope, as you may use too much or too little of the blender fluid at first. Each copy can only be used to make one transfer. Be sure to work in a well-ventilated area.

5. Cut out the image you want to transfer, leaving a good border around it. Tape it lightly to your envelope, face down.

Go over the back of it with your blender pen until it becomes translucent and you can see the image. Then use a bone folder or the handle of your scissors to rub all over the image several times. Lift off the paper, and your image will be transferred onto the envelope.

6. Your transfers may be colored in with colored pencil or watercolor, if you wish. You may also add rubber-stamped words to your envelope.

sunny flowers

Layer pretty petals for a paper garden

Maricel Fabi

what you need

Tool Box (page 12)

Template (page 112)

White and yellow card stock

Small and medium flower punches

Glue pen

Commercial envelope

7 white and 34 yellow rhinestones

Organza ribbon

Finished Size
6⅛ x 5 inches
(15.6 x 12.7 cm)

what you do

1. Using the template, cut out seven yellow and 34 white flowers from the card stock. Punch out 34 small and 20 medium flowers from white card stock. Punch out seven small and 21 medium flowers from yellow card stock. Adjust the number of flowers needed depending on your envelope size.

2. Assemble the flowers by layering one large, one medium, and one small flower—mixing and matching the colors. Glue each layer together at the center.

3. Glue the finished flowers to the envelope. Glue white and yellow rhinestones in the center of each flower, as desired. Let dry.

4. Curl out flower petals for a more dimensional effect.

5. Fasten the envelope by wrapping it with the organza ribbon.

Tip
After gluing the flowers to the envelope, you can fill any spaces between them with additional small flowers.

33

top secret

Elizabeth Nolin Pickett

Finished Size
4⅜ x 5¾ inches
(11.1 x 14.6 cm)

what you do

1. Unfold a privacy-patterned envelope, pulling open all glued edges, and lay flat.

2. On white paper, trace around the envelope template (page 000) and cut it out. Place the template on top of the privacy envelope, trace, and then cut out.

3. Draw lines on the plain side of your envelope (using a straight edge) from indented corner to indented corner. Fold along these lines—side flaps first, then bottom and top flaps.

4. Trace and cut out the envelope liner template (page 000), using teal-colored paper. Use the glue stick to coat the back of the liner paper with glue; then center the sides and bottom onto the interior of the envelope. You will notice that there is a wider edge on the envelope flap than on the liner paper. Because you apply the glue to this wider edge when sealing the flap, the inner lining is protected from tearing when your recipient opens the envelope.

5. Fold in the envelope sides, and use the glue stick to seal them together where they meet. Then put glue along the two edges of the bottom flap and fold it up to seal.

6. Use a blank self-stick label to create an area for the mailing address (and the return address, if desired).

dress
& address

Stitch
paper
frocks—
one size
fits all!

Mar
Goman

Finished Size
Envelope: 7¼ x 5¼ inches (18.4 x 13.3 cm)
Card: 5 x 7 inches (12.7 x 17.8 cm)

what you do

1. Gather some papers together for your dresses. Try cutting paintings out of old art books or photos out of other old books. You can also use old typewritten or handwritten letters, which you can age by staining them with ink or thinned paint. Dip a paper towel in the ink and rub it on the surface of the paper in an irregular pattern.

2. Make scrap-paper patterns for little dresses sized to fit your envelopes and cards. Trace these onto the back of the papers you want to use and cut them out.

3. To sew a dress directly onto an envelope, you will need to take the envelope apart by opening the glued seams. Do this by slipping a needle tool in the seam and sliding it along slowly.

4. Glue the dress lightly to the paper. Then place the envelope or card with the dress on a soft surface, such as a straw coaster or a piece of foam core. With a needle tool or a largish needle, punch holes along the edge of the dress through the backing. It is much easier to sew on paper if you pre-punch the holes, so don't skip this step.

5. Sew the dress on, using a regular needle and thread. Start sewing on the front side, leaving a tail of thread; when you finish sewing, you can tie the two tails together and let them hang down for added interest.

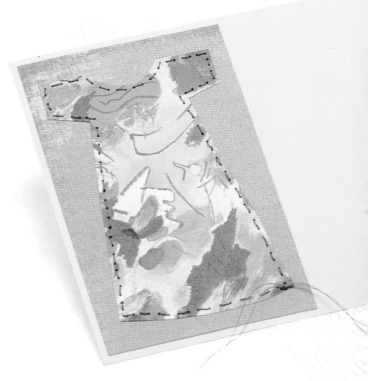

Variations

Cut a piece of coordinating colored paper to fit the end of the envelope and sew the dress onto this first. Then you can glue the paper onto the envelope without taking the envelope apart.

For matching cards, use the same techniques. Try setting eyelets in the corners for added interest. You can sew directly onto the card, or onto a colored paper that can then be glued on or attached to the front of the card with eyelets and glue. Buttons or other accents may be sewed on as well.

SURPRISING supplies

chapter 2

It's an encyclopedia.
It's a sweater. It's an envelope!
The most unusual materials
become the most
creative packaging.

Missionary Object Lessons

FOR

*Primary Departments of Sunday-schools,
Junior Societies and Mission Bands.*

¶ The very best material in the life and
literature of home and foreign missions is
now being made available for use in
teaching children under nine years of age.

¶ The story method enables the teachers
to utilize the customs of strange peoples
living in strange lands as the background
for teaching a missionary lesson.

¶ Pictures always delight children. They
never tire of hearing stories and seeing
pictures of other children.

¶ Objects add concreteness to the material of the story.

HOGARTH
Lord Lovat

smart sack

Give grocery bags a vintage chic makeover

Sharon Rohloff

what you need

Tool Box (page 12)

Paper grocery sack

Unfolded commercial envelope or template, page 113

Vintage wallpaper or patterned paper

Decorative scissors

Gold leafing pen

Rubber stamp of a mailing label

Card stock or scrapbooking paper

Tape

Old postage stamp

Glue stick

Sewing machine

Thread in a contrasting color

Double-sided tape

Ribbon, any type and size

Finished Size

Envelope: 7 ¼ x 5 ½ inches (18.4 x 14 cm)

Note card: 7 x 5 inches (17.8 x 12.7 cm)

what you do

For the Envelope

1. To make the envelope, first open up a paper grocery sack. Lay it blank side up with the envelope template on top. Trace around the template with the pencil and cut out the envelope. Turn it over to the printed side (this will be the inside of the envelope) and fold the side flaps inward.

2. Unfold the paper bag envelope and lay it down with the blank side up. Slide a 2 x 5½-inch (5.1 x 14 cm) wallpaper piece (face down) under the right-side flap. Trace the envelope edge onto the wallpaper. Cut the wallpaper to match the envelope shape. Fold the wallpaper around the envelope edge to make assembly easier. Use decorative scissors on the edge that will fold over the envelope face. Color the cut edge of the wallpaper with the gold leafing pen. Set this piece of wallpaper aside.

3. To create the flap embellishment, lay the envelope form blank side up on a 7 ¼ x 2½-inch (18.4 x 6.4) wallpaper scrap, also blank side up. Trace the edges of the envelope flap onto the wallpaper. Cut the wallpaper to match the envelope curves.

4. Stamp a mailing label on card stock or scrapbook paper and cut it out.

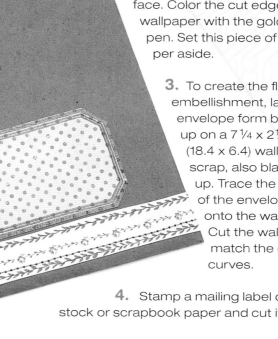

5. With decorative scissors, cut a 4½ x ¾-inch (11.4 x 1.9 cm) strip of wallpaper for embellishment below the mailing label. Color the ¾-inch (1.9 cm) edges with the gold leafing pen.

6. To assemble, tape the wallpaper cutouts to the left side and flap of the paper bag to make sewing easier. Adhere the mailing label and old postage stamp with the glue stick. Glue the strip of wallpaper below the mailing label. Sew the wallpaper to the envelope, using contrasting thread.

7. Fold the side flaps in. Fold the bottom flap up and adhere it to the sides with double-sided tape. Fold the top flap down to use.

For the Matching Stationery

1. Cut a piece of 5 x 7-inch (12.7 x 17.8 cm) card stock. Then cut a 9 x 7-inch (22.9 x 17.8 cm) piece of wallpaper from the same paper you used for the envelope. Trim the top and

bottom edges of the wallpaper with decorative scissors. Rub the gold leafing pen over the cut edges.

2. Lay the wallpaper patterned side down. Center the card stock on the wallpaper, and fold the left edge ½ inch (1.3 cm) in toward the card stock. Fold another ½ inch (1.3 cm) over the edge of the card stock. Adhere the wallpaper to the card stock with glue. Repeat with the wallpaper on the right side of the card stock.

3. Before folding the top and bottom edges of the wallpaper over the card stock, notch the corners of the wallpaper on the diagonal to make folding easier.

4. Fold the top edge down and the bottom edge up. Adhere the flaps to the card stock with glue. Sew around the entire border using a sewing machine and contrasting thread.

5. Punch two holes at the top of the stationery. Put the ribbon through the holes and tie it into a bow.

patchwork garden

love from
THE GIRLS INSTITUTE

INSTIT

Fiona Hesford

what you need

Tool Box (page 12)

Commercial envelope (for template)

Fine-point black marker pen

4 color copies of floral fabric patterns, each 8½ x 11 inches (21.6 x 27.9 cm)

Glue

Paper clips

Pink embroidery thread and a sharp needle

Small pink button, ½ inch (1.3 cm) in diameter

Decorative scissors with a zigzag edge

A sheet of white paper

Template (page 114)

Finished Size
Envelope: 7¼ x 4¾ inches
(18.4 x 12.1 cm)
Card: 4¼ x 6 inches
(10.8 x 15.2 cm)

Tips
Pick your fabric patterns with care. The aim is to get a medley of patterns in harmony with one another. Small design motifs work best.

You can scan the fabrics and print them, or take digital photos of the patterns and print them.

what you do

Making the Envelope

1. Open out the commercial envelope into a template, being careful not to tear it. This one is 7¼ x 4¾ inches (18.4 x 12.1 cm), but you could use other sizes.

2. Cut the envelope with scissors along the four folded sides so you have five pieces: top flap (A), bottom flap (B), side flaps (C) and (D), and base (E).

3. Using these pieces as templates, draw around the shapes on the plain side of the pattern copies. For each piece, use a different pattern (except the side pieces, which are both in the same pattern). Cut two of piece (A).

4. Glue the plain sides of the two (A) pieces together.

5. Hold the pieces together with paper clips in the same arrangement as the original envelope. This will secure them in place while you sew the pieces together.

6. With the needle and embroidery thread, sew a blanket stitch all around the outside edge of the envelope and top flap.

7. Cut a slit for a buttonhole on the top flap with the craft knife on a cutting mat, or use small, sharp-pointed scissors to make the slit instead.

8. Sew on a cute button in the corresponding position on the back of the envelope, with the buttonhole on the opposite side.

9. Type or write a message or address on a piece of the left-over patterned paper. Then cut around it with zigzag scissors to make a rectangle measuring approximately 4 x 2 inches (10.2 x 5.1 cm). Sew a running stitch around the edge with the same thread as before. Glue the label to the front of the envelope.

Making the Card

1. Using the dress template, cut two shapes out of patterned paper and glue them together, plain sides facing. Carefully outline the shape with a fine black marker pen. Remember that if your envelope size varies from the one shown, you will need to adjust your card size accordingly.

2. Type or write your message on white paper, then cut around it with zigzag scissors so the rectangle measures approximately 3 x 2¼ inches (7.6 x 5.7 cm). If your card is larger or smaller than the one shown, you may need to adjust the size of the rectangle.

3. Glue your message to the front of the card. There you have it: one lovely patchwork envelope and card to match!

Please come to
THE GIRLS INSTITUTES
CHARITY GARDEN
CRAFT FAIR
on
Sunday 24th Aug 08
from 2-4pm

crafts. cakes.
lots of lovely
stuff!

THE GIRLS

Tip
For a charming, old-fashioned look, use a vintage typewriter to type your message or address label.

tea cozy

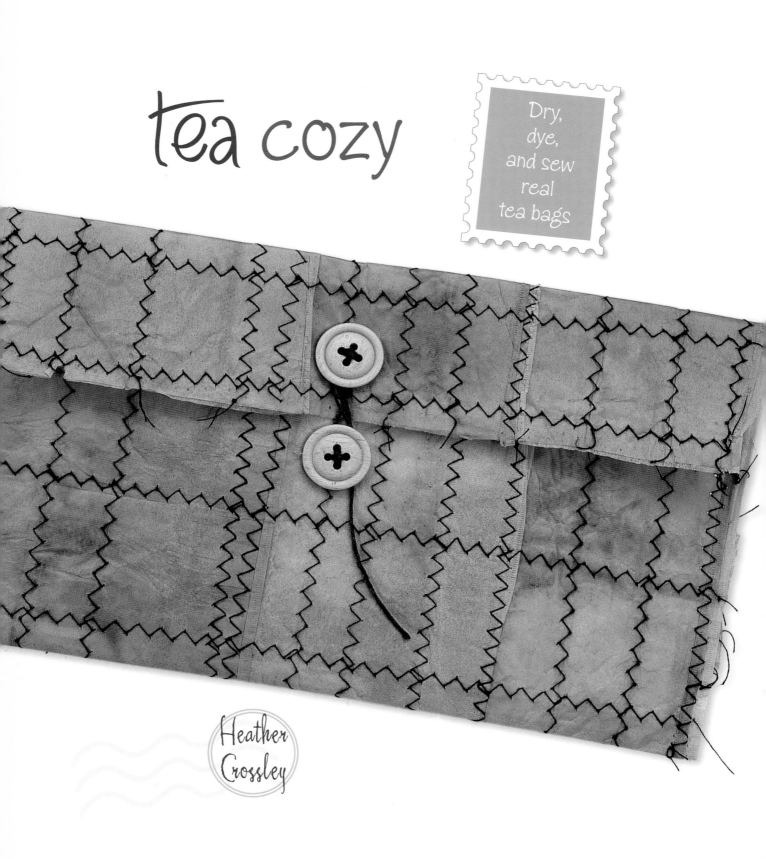

Heather Crossley

what you need

Tool Box (page 12)

12 used tea bags

Sewing machine

Black thread

2 tan buttons

Black linen thread, 7 inches (17.8 cm) long

Hand sewing needle

Finished Size
8½ x 4¾ inches
(21.6 x 12.1 cm)

what you do

1. Dry out used tea bags. When they are dry, gently remove the staple holding each bag together and discard the tea leaves. Carefully open the seam so you have a single sheet; then smooth out the tea bag paper.

2. A regular-size tea bag is about 5½ x 3½ inches (14 x 8.9 cm). Your tea bags may be a slightly different size, but that's okay. To create this envelope, you will need to stitch a double layer of tea bags together to make an approximately 11 x 8¼-inch (27.9 x 21 cm) sheet. You need a double layer because tea bag paper is very delicate.

3. Place two of the tea bags together, one on top of the other, to form the double layer. Place another set of doubled tea bags next to the first, overlapping them by about ¾ inch (1.9 cm) at the edges.

4. Join the tea bags together by sewing right down the strip where the edges overlap, using a zigzag stitch in black thread. Take your time with the sewing, making sure that the tea bags are lined up straight.

5. Just before reaching about ¾ inch (1.9 cm) from the bottom edge of the tea bags, place two more sets of doubled tea bags under the first two, with their top edges at the point where you stopped sewing (creating another overlap of ¾ inch [1.9 cm]), and continue stitching to the bottom of these additional tea bags. Now you have an 11 x 5½-inch (27.9 x 14 cm) sheet.

Tip

Don't worry about knotting the ends of the machine-sewn threads; let your piece look unique.

6. Place another double layer of tea bags next to the top two, overlapping slightly (you'll have a row of three across), and stitch down as before.

7. Again, before reaching ¾ inch (1.9 cm) from the bottom, overlap another set of doubled tea bags and continue stitching to the bottom of the additional tea bags. Now you have an 11 x 8¼-inch (27.9 x 21 cm) sheet, made of two rows of three doubled tea bag papers.

8. Once you have the structure and size of the piece completed, begin zigzag stitching together the length and width of the whole piece, especially where the tea bag papers join. However, avoid stitching down the lengthwise edges just yet. If you like, you can use a different stitch pattern from the one shown.

9. When completed, fold the piece to create an envelope with the top edge about 3 inches (7.6 cm) above the bottom edge.

10. With the flap open, stitch down the lengthwise edges to create the pocket of the envelope.

11. With black thread, delicately hand stitch the two buttons onto the envelope to create the closure. For the tie to join the two buttons together, stitch a piece of black linen thread neatly to the back of the button on the flap of the envelope.

wintery remix

Salvage cool wrapping paper scraps

Amy Jean
Rowan

Tool Box (page 12)

Template (page 115)

Vellum paper, heavyweight

Wrapping paper

Glue stick or wafer seal

Vintage gummed label

Card stock suitable for ink-jet printer (optional)

Finished Size

Envelope: 5⅛ x 3⅝ inches (13 x 9.2 cm)

Card: 4⅞ x 3½ inches (12.4 x 8.9 cm)

what you do

1. Photocopy the envelope template. Trace it onto the heavyweight vellum. Use heavyweight vellum so you can see through it to compose your envelope. Cut the vellum template out so you can easily trace around it.

2. Place the template on the wrapping paper where it looks the best and trace the shape. Cut out the envelope.

3. Flip the envelope over to the blank side. Make four score lines with the ruler, where the flaps meet up with the face of the envelope. Refer to the template for position.

4. Gently fold each flap in, and release the top and bottom flaps.

5. Noting the orientation of your pattern on the front, find the bottom flap of your envelope and glue it to the side flaps. Do this by coating the left and right sides of the bottom flap about ¼ inch (6 mm) from the edge; then fold to close.

6. Wet the gummed label and adhere to the front for addressing. You can also use a self-adhesive mailing label.

7. To create a matching card, scan a piece of the art from the wrapping paper and print it onto card stock on the ink-jet printer. Be sure to leave ample room for a holiday message.

8. Use a glue stick or wafer seal to seal the envelope. Add a first-class stamp and send!

peep show

Expose all through a clear acrylic window

hello baby

winter wonderland · winter wonderland · winter wonderland · winter wonderland · winter wonderland

597856123 24698765 132 120

baby, it's cold outside!

Cathy Schellenberg

what you need

Tool Box (page 12)

Template (page 116)

White paper or card stock

Card stock or patterned paper, 8½ x 11 inches
(21.6 x 27.9 cm)

Acrylic sheet, 5 x 4 inches (12.7 x 10.2 cm)

Paper adhesive

Glue stick

Various rub-ons and pens

Craft sealant

Finished Size
5¾ x 4½ inches
(14.6 x 11.4 cm)

what you do

1. Photocopy the envelope template (page 116) onto a plain white piece of paper. If you want to use it over and over, you may want to copy it onto something heavy (card stock) that will withstand being handled a lot.

2. Place the template onto the patterned paper and cut around it with scissors. An alternative is to trace around the template with pencil or print it onto the white side of the patterned paper, but then the template lines may show on the inside of the envelope.

3. Fold up the flaps on the envelope, but before gluing the envelope together, lay the envelope flat on a cutting mat (pattern side up), and, with a craft knife, measure and cut a hole in the front of the envelope, slightly smaller than your acrylic piece.

4. Using a strong glue or paper adhesive, attach your piece of acrylic, trimmed slightly larger than the opening, inside the opening on the front of the envelope.

5. Apply glue along the side flaps of the envelope with a glue stick, fold them down, and then fold the bottom flap up to make the pocket.

6. Decorate the front of the envelope as desired with rub-ons, stickers, doodling, and so on. Keep embellishments flat, and even use a coat of craft sealant if the envelope will be sent through the mail. If you're hand delivering the card and envelope, embellishments may include bulkier items (flowers or buttons, for example).

Tips
Write your recipient's mailing address on a small piece of paper and slip it into the envelope window.

Position your card inside so its sentiment is visible through the window.

hot off the press

Melony Bradley

what you need

Tool Box (page 12)

Old encyclopedia volume

Template (page 117)

Craft glue

Large foam stamp with a floral, leaf, or other design

Rubber stamp with a shoe, butterfly, message, or other design

Watermark ink

Embossing powder (red, black, or other colors as desired)

Heat tool

Embellishments, such as coordinating stickers, silk flowers,
    decorative brads, self-adhesive rhinestones, or card stock
    printed with a design

Finished Size
4⅛ x 5 inches
(10.5 x 12.7 cm)

what you do

1. Remove a page from the encyclopedia by cutting along the spine with the craft knife. Use the template provided to trace with the pencil on one side of the page. Cut out with the scissors and score along the lines indicated, folding the left and right side flaps in first. Glue the left and right edges inside the bottom flap to the bottom of the left and right envelope flaps. Score the remaining top flap inward.

2. Ink the large foam image with the watermark ink. Stamp the right side of the envelope, with the image bleeding off the edge. Sprinkle with colored embossing powder and remove any excess. Heat the image with the heat tool. Allow to dry.

3. Ink the rubber stamp image with the watermark ink and stamp on top of the first image. Sprinkle the image with a different color of embossing powder. Emboss and allow to dry.

4. Add a three-dimensional embellishment, such as a silk flower. Layer the silk flowers together and insert the brad. Glue to the envelope. You can also add a decorative strip of card stock down the left-hand side. Cut a narrow rectangle, approximately the height of the card, 4⅛ x ¾ inches (10.5 x 1.9 cm) from the card stock and glue vertically, close to the left-hand edge of the envelope. Use stickers, self-adhesive rhinestones, and additional card stock to complete your creation.

peel-n-stick

Convert contact paper into custom packaging

Joan K. Morris

54

what you need

Tool Box (page 12)

Templates (pages 118–119)

Glue stick

Small hole punch

Industrial-strength clear glue

Toothpick

Wire cutters

For the Wood-Grain Envelope

Scrap paper for pattern, 16 x 20
   inches (40.6 x 50.8 cm)

Wood-grain contact paper
   (shelf liner with adhesive)

Plain white paper, 16 x 20 inches
   (40.6 x 50.8 cm)

Brown waxed linen thread,
   20 inches (50.8 cm) long

Two 1-inch (2.5 cm) wooden
   buttons with two holes

For the Faux Aluminum Envelope

Scrap paper for pattern, 16 x 16
   inches (40.6 x 40.6 cm)

Faux aluminum contact paper
   (shelf liner with adhesive)

Plain white paper, 16 x 16 inches
   (40.6 x 40.6 cm)

Washer, ⅝ inch (1.6 cm)

Nut, ⅜ inch (9.5 mm)

28-gauge silver wire, 1½ yards
   (1.4 m) long

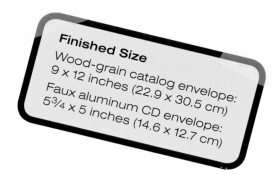

Finished Size

Wood-grain catalog envelope:
9 x 12 inches (22.9 x 30.5 cm)

Faux aluminum CD envelope:
5¾ x 5 inches (14.6 x 12.7 cm)

what you do

Making the Wood-Grain Envelope

1. On the scrap paper, make a pattern for the envelope from the template provided (page 118). Cut the pattern out.

2. With the pencil, trace all the way around the edge of the cutout pattern piece onto the 16 x 20-inch (40.6 x 50.8 cm) plain paper.

3. Cut a 16 x 20-inch (40.6 x 50.8 cm) piece of the wood-grain contact paper, with the paper backing in place.

4. Place the piece of plain white paper, with the outline drawing facing up, on the sticky side of the contact paper. The best way to do this is to remove half of the paper backing, set the outline paper in position, and smooth the paper down as you remove the rest of the paper backing. Use the bone folder to smooth out any wrinkles.

5. Cut out the shape drawn on the plain paper. Cut close to the pencil line. Erase any pencil lines that remain.

6. Fold and crease the envelope following the template. Fold the side edges in first and then the bottom and then the top. It helps to keep the edges of the fold straight if you place a flat ruler along the line to be folded and fold the edge up over the ruler. Use the bone folder to flatten the fold.

7. Fold the two sides together and glue them together with the glue stick. Fold up the bottom and glue it down with the glue stick. Let the envelope sit for 20 minutes or so to allow the glue to dry.

8. Decide where you want to place your two buttons, one on the top flap and one just below the flap, and mark the spots with the pencil. Mark both holes in each button too.

9. Cut two 1 x 1-inch (2.5 x 2.5 cm) pieces of the contact paper. Remove the paper backing, and place one of the squares on the inside of the upper flap under where you have marked for the button. This will give the buttons extra support. The other square will go under the other button after it has been tied in position to hide the ends of the thread.

10. Punch out the dots you've marked for the buttonholes with the small hole punch. Cut a piece of the brown waxed linen thread 6 inches

(15.2 cm) long. Run this thread through the front holes of one of the buttons and center the thread. Run both ends of the thread through the two holes on the body of the envelope to the inside. Tie a double knot and cut off the ends. Place the other square of contact paper over the knot.

11. To place the button on the flap, use the rest of the waxed linen. Run the waxed linen thread up through the holes on the inside of the flap through the button. Tie a double knot on top of the button, leaving one end of the waxed linen thread 8 inches (20.3 cm) long and cutting the other end off.

12. Place a dab of industrial-strength glue on the knot to keep it in place. Let the glue dry.

13. To use the waxed linen thread for the closure, wrap the thread back and forth around the buttons.

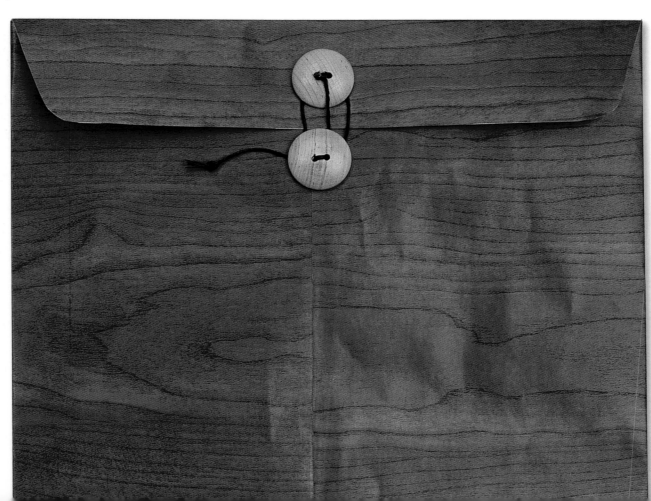

Making the Faux Aluminum Envelope

1. On the scrap paper, make a pattern from the template provided (page 119). Cut the pattern out.

2. With the pencil, draw around the pattern onto the 16 x 16-inch (40.6 x 40.6 cm) plain white paper.

3. Cut a 16 x 16-inch (40.6 x 40.6 cm) piece of the aluminum-look contact paper, with the paper backing in place.

4. Place the plain paper, with the outline drawing facing up, onto the sticky side of the contact paper. Do this by removing half the paper backing, placing the outline paper in position, and smoothing the paper down as you remove the rest of the paper backing. Use the bone folder to smooth out any wrinkles.

5. Cut out the shape drawn on the plain paper. Cut close to the pencil line. Erase any pencil lines that remain.

6. Fold and crease the envelope, following the template. Fold the side edges in first and then the bottom and then the top. Use the bone folder to flatten the folds.

7. Following the manufacturer's instructions, use the industrial-strength clear glue to glue the side flaps together. With a toothpick, place a dab of the glue between the flaps and press the flaps together. Bring the bottom flap up. This will show you where to place dabs of the glue on the side flaps to hold the bottom flap. Glue the bottom flap; then let the glue dry.

8. Glue the nut to the washer with the industrial-strength glue. Let the glue dry.

9. To give some extra strength to the top flap, add a piece of the aluminum contact paper to the inside of the flap. To do this, cut a piece of the contact paper to 6 x 6 inches (15.2 x 15.2 cm).

Remove the paper backing and place it sticky side down on the inside of the top flap, lining up with the fold. Cut around the edge, matching the original flap.

10. Punch two holes in the top flap where marked on the template. Mark through these two holes onto the bottom and side flaps and punch out those marks.

11. With the envelope flap side up, center the 28-gauge wire on the back of the envelope and bring the ends to the front (the flap side). Run each end of the wire through one hole on the bottom flap and out the other. Bring the two ends of the wire up through the holes in the top flap and thread them through the washer and nut. Run one wire end to the back of the envelope and around in one direction, and then run the other end in the other direction. Bring them to the front and wrap them once around the washer and nut to hold in place.

sweeter sweaters

FROM ME

TO YOU

FOR YOU

Sarah Lightfoot-Brundage

58

what you need

Tool Box (page 12)

One or two 100-percent wool sweaters, each a different color

Craft paper (for pattern, optional)

Sewing machine

Thread for sewing, in a contrasting color

Plain fabric, such as cotton or linen, 12 x 12 inches
  (30.5 x 30.5 cm)

Letter stamps

Ink pad

Waxed linen cord, 24 inches (61 cm) total

Darning or similar needle, large enough for the waxed linen

Two buttons with holes large enough for the needle

Pins

Finished Size
7 x 7 inches
(17.8 x 17.8 cm)

what you do

1. Shrink one or two wool sweaters by washing in hot water. Thrift shop sweaters are ideal, and a great way to repurpose. Use two different colors for more interest.

2. Cut a 7 x 7-inch (17.8 x 17.8 cm) square from one wool sweater. Cut a pentagon shape from another sweater of a different color. The square portion of the pentagon shape should match the first square in size, 7 x 7 inches (17.8 x 17.8 cm), and the triangle portion of the pentagon, which will form the flap of the envelope, should be approximately 4 inches (10.2 cm) in height. (If you wish, you can make patterns for cutting using craft paper.)

3. On each piece, use a sewing machine to stitch a random pattern in a decorative stitch of your choice. The thread should be in a contrasting color to your sweater color. You may choose to stitch a flower design instead. If you do, begin the center of the flower $3/8$ inch (9.5 mm) to $1/2$ inch (1.3 cm) below the center, approximately $4 1/2$ inches (11.4 cm) from the top of the piece. Your button or center needs to sit this far down to properly be tied to the button on the flap.

4. On the pentagon piece, stitch by machine around the point to reinforce the edge.

5. Cut out two decorative labels from linen or other plain fabric of your choice. The shapes of these labels are optional. However, the label for the back flap must be small enough to fit in the triangular space. With letter stamps and an ink stamp pad, spell out your message onto the fabric. Allow a few minutes for the ink to dry.

6. Sew the labels in place on the pentagon piece, one on the center front and the other on what will be the back flap of your envelope. With the pentagon piece in front of you, be sure the label on the back flap is placed upside down, so when the flap closes, the message will read correctly.

7. Using linen cord and a large needle, sew the button to the square piece, $3/8$ inch (9.5 mm) to $1/2$ inch (1.3 cm) below the center. Knot it on the underside of the wool piece.

Variation
These instructions are for a CD-sized envelope. You can alter the pattern sizes to fit a small notebook or other item.

8. To affix a second button to the point of the pentagon piece, begin by threading a needle with a 12-inch (30.5 cm) length of linen cord. Stitch the button to the point, leaving an 8-inch (20.3 cm) tail on the outside. To finish off, knot the cord and tail under the button and trim the cord—but not the tail. The long tail will wrap around the other button to keep your envelope closed.

9. Pin the pieces together, wrong sides facing. Sew with a straight stitch along each side and the bottom only. Don't worry if the sweater pieces don't line up exactly. They move and slide a bit, and remember, the wool gives and stretches. You can trim the sewn edges later if necessary.

10. Once you have sewn your envelope together, insert a CD, notebook, or other item of your choice. Fold over the flap. Wind the cord around both buttons.

loose leaf

Sculpt and seal a translucent tea bag

PLEASE SEND to:
MISS VICTORINE BELLOQ
P.O. BOX 315
NEW YORK, NEW YORK 10013

USA 39

WASHINGTON
NATIONAL CAPITAL
SESQUICENTENNIAL
1800-1950

Jennie
Hinchcliff

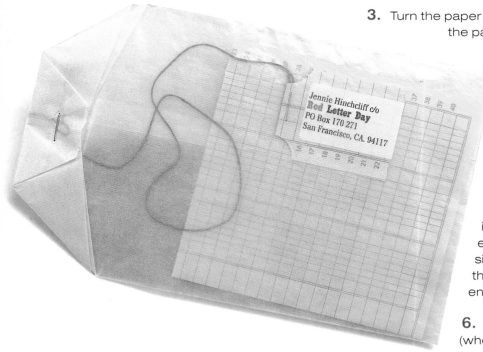

what you need

Tool Box (page 12)

Sheet of glassine or vellum, 20 x 10 inches (50.8 x 25.4 cm)

Glue stick

Materials to write letter or make card

Loose-leaf tea to include inside envelope

Decorative paper for envelope return address label,
   4 x 1⅝ inches (10.2 x 4.1 cm)

Twine or embroidery floss, 10 inches (25.4 cm) long

Stapler

Finished Size
7½ x 4¾ inches
(19 x 12.1 cm)

what you do

1. With the piece of glassine or vellum paper in a landscape position, score a horizontal line with the bone folder 3 inches (7.6 cm) from the bottom edge. Fold the paper along this line upward from the bottom.

2. From the top edge, measure down 2¼ inches (5.7 cm) and score a horizontal line with the bone folder. Fold down from the top along this line. The top edge now overlaps the bottom edge slightly; glue the edges together along the overlap.

3. Turn the paper over with the seam side down and the paper still in the landscape position. Fold the right-hand edge over to the left-hand edge. Crease with the bone folder.

4. Measure in ⅝ inch (1.6 cm) from the creased edge; score a vertical line with the bone folder. Fold the top piece from left to right along this line.

5. Turn the paper over, measure in ⅝ inch (1.6 cm) from the creased edge again, and fold back the other side to match the first. This completes the expandable bottom of your tea bag envelope.

6. From the bottom of your envelope (where the creased edges are), measure

Jennie Hinchcliff c/o
Red Letter Day
PO Box 170 271
San Francisco, CA. 94117

8½ inches (21.6 cm); trim off all layers of paper to this length. Then measure 8 inches (20.3 cm) from the bottom and trim off only the top two layers of paper to this length, leaving the bottom two layers at 8½ inches (21.6 cm).

7. Working with the top edge of your envelope, fold the left-hand corner over so that it forms a triangular shape; repeat on the right-hand side. Fold your two triangles to make their points meet in the middle, and leave approximately ½ inch (1.3 cm) unfolded in the middle of the top of your envelope—this makes the envelope look more like a tea bag when folded over.

8. Fold the topmost edge over so that the horizontal edge you left in step 7 is just below the meeting point of the two triangles. Crease with the bone folder.

9. Set the envelope aside. Write a letter or create a card. Then carefully unfold the top edge of the envelope and slip your missive inside one of the layers that form the envelope.

10. In the remaining layer, carefully pour loose-leaf tea. Remember, the envelope will have to make its way through a lot of complicated post office machinery, so try to keep the contents as flat as possible.

11. To create a return address label, fold the 4 x 1⅝-inch (10.2 x 4.1 cm) piece of decorative paper in half vertically.

12. Using a coin, cut two rounded pieces away from the top corners of the return address label. Be sure the pieces being cut away are from the creased edge!

13. Sandwich the piece of twine inside the folded return address label. Staple to hold in place. Handwrite the return address or apply an address label.

14. Carefully unfold the top opening of your envelope; tuck the return address label inside, in the layer with the tea. Making sure that a tiny tail of twine is sticking out of the top of envelope, refold and staple closed.

15. Affix the address label and postage. Add other surface decoration if desired, and you're ready to mail your creation!

daily grind

PLEASE SEND to:
M. SEBASTIAN ABELARD
7961 N.E. AVENUE WEST
NEW YORK, NEW YORK 10013

Jennie Hinchcliff

what you need

Tool Box (page 12)

Paper coffee filters used for automatic-drip coffee makers

Coffee, tea, or sepia-colored ink, for paper dyeing

Dressmaker's tracing wheel

Needle and thread (or sewing machine)

Self-stick address label

what you do

1. Dye two coffee filters using coffee, tea, or ink. Filters do not have to be left in the dye bath for very long, but be sure to let them dry thoroughly. Filters should be a warm brown color, reminiscent of cappuccino or café latte.

2. Using a dressmaker's tracing wheel, perforate one of the filters from edge to edge, about one-third of the way down from the top. The person who receives your mail will open it along this perforation.

3. Stitch both coffee filters together by hand (or sewing machine). Be sure to stitch approximately ¼ inch (6 mm) from the outside edge. Do not sew all the way around the diameter of the filters—leave an opening of 4 to 5 inches (10.2 to 12.7 cm). Once you have created your card or written a letter, slip it inside your envelope and stitch closed. Once stitched together, the two filters will form a single envelope.

4. Affix an address label and postage. Add other surface decoration if you wish, and put your coffee envelope in the mailbox!

torch song

Shape, heat, and adorn copper mesh

Mary Hettmansperger

what you need

Tool Box (page 12)

144 x 144-gauge copper mesh, 6 x 6 inches (15.2 x 15.2 cm)

Needle-nose pliers

Propane torch

Copper foil, .002 thickness, 2 x 3 inches (5.1 x 7.6 cm)

Tin snips or sheet metal cutters

Decorative paper, card stock weight

Mica, 3 x 4 inches (7.6 x 10.2 cm)

Drill and 1/16 bit or mini metal hole punch

Small scrapbooking brads

24-gauge copper wire, 1 to 2 feet (30.5 to 61 cm)

Finished Size
4 x 3¼ inches
(10.2 x 8.3 cm)

what you do

1. Bend each side of the copper mesh over ¹⁄₁₆ inch (1.6 mm) to make a selvage edge and eliminate the sharp mesh edge. Use the ruler to bend the mesh up and to keep the line straight. Make sure to bend the mesh tightly. You can burnish the edge lightly or use pliers to secure it.

2. Use a propane torch to add a heat patina. Turn the torch on and hold it about 3 to 5 inches (7.6 to 12.7 cm) away from the mesh. Move it lightly over the surface to create color swirls and patterns. Don't hold the flame in one area for too long, or the heat could turn the copper black or even burn through it.

3. Turn the piece of mesh so the selvage edges are face up. Measure 2 inches (5.1 cm) from one of the corners toward the center of the square, and mark a fold line across the mesh with a pencil. Bend the corner along the line. Set the mesh aside.

4. Take the copper foil and cut into one side to make strips about ⅛ to ¼-inch (3 to 6 mm) wide, leaving them connected on the other side, much like fringe.

5. Cut strips out of decorative paper about the same width as the copper strips, and a little longer than the width of the entire copper fringe. Weave the paper strips into the copper fringe with an over/under weave, letting the extra hang out the ends.

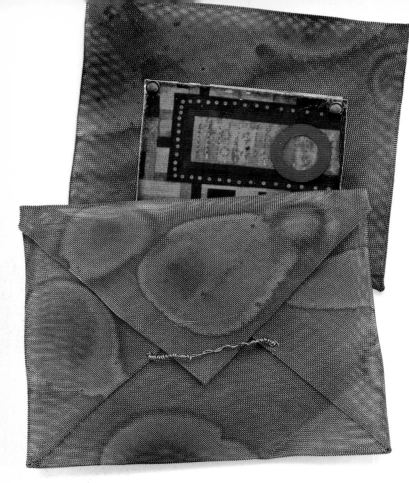

6. Fold the solid, connected side of the copper piece and the ends of the fringe copper to the back side of the woven piece. Cut the extra lengths of paper even with the edge of the copper.

7. Using sharp scissors, cut the mica into a rectangle a little wider and longer than the woven copper grid. Make sure it still fits in the area of the envelope.

8. Drill or punch a hole in each corner of the mica. You may want to add two more holes in the center of the longer sides of the rectangle to make sure the mica will completely fasten to the mesh.

9. Center the woven grid on the front of the envelope. Place the mica over the copper woven grid. Insert the brads through the holes in the mica and copper mesh. Open the brads on the inside to secure. If the brad does not go through the mesh easily, bore out the hole with a tapestry needle to ease it through.

10. Use the propane torch to burn one end of the 24-gauge wire, creating a ball on the end. Set aside.

11. Lay down the copper mesh with the copper grid face down and the fold you made in step 3 at the bottom. Bend in the left and right corners of the mesh to meet the bottom triangle. The bottom edges of the left and right triangles should overlap the bottom triangle just enough to make a good connection. (See how the triangles meet in the photo to the left.)

12. Take the end of the 24-gauge wire without the ball and begin stitching the bottom flap to the left flap, starting at the point of the left flap. Stitch about ½ inch (1.3 cm) down the left flap and then out of the envelope.

13. Lay the wire across to the right flap. (See the photo at left again.) Leave this wire a little loose.

14. Stitch the wire to connect the right flap and the bottom triangle as in step 12, except this time you're working from about ½ inch (1.3 cm) below the point of the right flap back up to the point. Bring the wire inside the envelope back to where the stitching began on the right flap and then through to the outside of the envelope. Wrap the wire tightly around the wire that you laid across the flaps in step 13. Trim any extra wire.

15. Notch the selvage on each side of the top flap to make it easier to fold down. Trim any extra copper off. If necessary, secure the edges of the selvage by burnishing or using pliers as in step 1. Fold down the top flap. The point needs to catch under the wrapped wire.

Variation: Using other metal mesh or screen gives you an entirely different look. You can also personalize the envelope by placing photographs, paper with text, or any flat item under the mica.

hold everything

The best way to send a gift is
inside another gift—craft
envelopes that do the trick!

small enterprise

Sharon Rohloff

Tool Box (page 12)

Patterned or printed paper,
   such as scrapbooking paper

Template (page 120)

Bone folder (optional)

Glue stick

Decorative sticker (optional)

Finished Size
3¾ x 2¼ inches
(9.5 x 5.7 cm)

what you do

1. Photocopy and place the template on the unprinted side of the paper and trace around it.

2. Carefully cut out the envelope shape, cutting just inside the lines so they don't show after assembly.

3. Place the envelope shape unprinted side up on the work surface and fold the two smaller flaps toward the center.

4. Fold the two larger flaps toward the center.

5. If desired, use a bone folder to sharpen the folds.

6. Unfold the two larger flaps and apply glue to the edges of the bottom flap where it overlaps the smaller flaps.

7. Refold the bottom flap into place, pressing firmly until the glue takes hold.

8. After inserting your business card or mini note card, either tuck the top flap underneath the bottom one or apply a decorative sticker to seal the envelope.

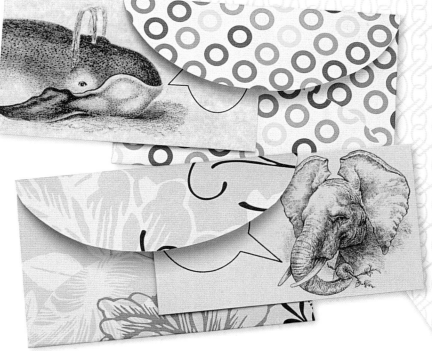

teeny
tags

Garnish gifts with beads and buttons

Johanna Chambers

72

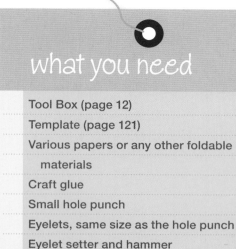

what you need

Finished Size
2 inches
(5.1 cm) tall

what you do

1. Using the template provided and scissors or a craft knife with a metal ruler, cut out the shape of the envelope from paper or other foldable material. Note that the top edge of the envelope may be cut into other shapes (such as a scalloped edge) to add interest. Be sure to cut out the envelope with the white (interior) side of the paper facing up.

2. Score and fold on the dashed lines. Glue the tab into the side of the envelope.

3. Cut out, score, and fold the card insert, and check that it fits the envelope.

4. Use the small hole punch to create a hole at the center of the top edge of the envelope.

Variations

Use unusual materials, such as chain or ribbon, for the loop. Try braiding a few different colors of cord into one loop. Experiment with more than one kind of paper, such as a two-sided or embossed variety. Try other foldable materials such as vellum or foil. Alter the shape at the top of the envelope. Use multiple eyelets or cutouts in the envelope. The sky's the limit!

5. Center an eyelet through the punched hole and affix it with the eyelet setter and hammer.

6. Make a loop of any kind of cord or wire and tie the ends together. Then use a lark's-head knot to secure the loop through the eyelet. You may want to add beads or knots to the loop for added detail.

7. Decorate the envelope with coordinating embellishments, such as beads, buttons, faux gems or flowers, or a cross-stitch pattern. Add to the design with paints, markers, or stamps.

you're gifted

Add dimension to the surprise inside

birthday wishes

Baby dear

Sharon Rohloff

Tool Box (page 12)

Double-sided patterned paper,
   card stock weight, 12 x 7 inches
   (30.5 x 17.8 cm)

Decorative scissors

Gold leafing pen

White card stock

Rubber stamp (for message)

Watermark ink pad

Embossing powder

Ink pad for pouncing

Leaf punch or scissors

Coordinating patterned paper

Glue stick

Large coin

Ribbon in two widths: ³⁄₈ inch
   (9.5 mm) and ³⁄₁₆ inch (5 mm)

Foam sticky dots

Dimensional flower stickers

Double-sided tape

Heat gun

Finished Size
4½ x 3½ inches
(11.4 x 8.9 cm)

what you do

1. Lay the piece of double-sided patterned card stock lengthwise and cut off a 4 x 1½-inch (10.2 x 3.8 cm) notch from both left corners. Cut a 3½ x 1½-inch (8.9 x 3.8 cm) notch from both right corners. You will end up with a cross-shaped band with a longer left-hand "flap."

2. Trim the ends of all flaps with decorative scissors. Color the cut edges with the gold pen. Fold the flaps toward the middle, starting with the top and bottom flaps. Next, fold the left and right flaps into the middle, with the right flap ending on top.

3. To create the tag, stamp your message on white card stock with watermark ink. Add embossing powder in a color of your choice and heat to emboss. Pounce ink on the tag, in a color that coordinates with the card stock design. Cut the tag out with decorative scissors. Color the edges with the gold leafing pen.

4. For the small leaves, blot a watermark ink pad on white paper. Add embossing powder and heat to create a rectangle of embossed paper. Cut four leaves from this embossed paper with a leaf punch or scissors. Set leaves aside to use in step 8.

5. Cut an 11½ x 2-inch (29.2 x 5.1 cm) band of patterned paper. Trim the ends with decorative scissors. Color the cut edges with the gold pen. Wrap it around the folded card holder to create creases. Center and adhere the paper band lengthwise to the outside of the card holder with the glue stick.

6. On the outside of the card holder, draw a light pencil line vertically where the right-side flap ends. Open the right side of the card holder. Center a large coin on the vertical line you have drawn. Trace a half circle on the right side of the vertical line. Open the card holder flat and cut along this line with a craft knife. This creates a tab to tuck the right flap under when the card holder is folded. Erase the pencil line.

7. Cut a 9-inch (22.9 cm) length of the ⅜-inch-wide (9.5 mm) ribbon. Center and adhere the ribbon to the left flap with glue, starting at the base of the tab. Fold the flaps inward. Tie a piece of the narrower ribbon in a bow around the other end of the ribbon and adhere to the card holder. Adhere the message tag to the right side of the bow with foam sticky dots.

8. Add a dimensional flower on top of the tab to conceal it. Tuck two leaves underneath the flower, pressing the flower sticker on them to adhere. Add two additional flowers with leaves along the ribbon band. Adhere the gift card to the inside of the card holder with double-sided tape.

dainty
charm

Joan K. Morris

what you need

Tool Box (page 12)

White lace piece, at least 8 1/2 x 11 inches
 (21.6 x 27.9 cm)

Hot pink and light pink paper, each 8 1/2 x 11
 inches (21.6 x 27.9 cm)

2 sheets of clear vellum paper, each 8 1/2 x 11
 inches (21.6 x 27.9 cm)

Color photocopier

Hot pink and light pink thread

Sewing machine

Clear tape

Hand sewing needle

Pink glass button, 5/8 inch (1.6 cm)

Round pink plastic button, 3/8 inch (1 cm)

Glue stick

Finished Size

Light pink envelope:
7 x 4 inches (17.8 x 10.2 cm)

Hot pink envelope:
4 1/4 x 4 1/4 inches (10.8 x 10.8 cm)

what you do

1.   Place the lace on the color photocopier face
down. Place the hot pink paper on top of the
lace. Close the lid of the copier and print onto the
vellum. Repeat with the other color paper. Let
the paper dry.

2.   Following the shape of your lace,
cut one 8 1/2-inch (21.6 cm) side of
each lace-printed vellum into the
flap shape. The shape you cut for
the flap will depend on your lace.

3. Cut the light pink vellum to approximately 7 x 11 inches (17.8 x 27.9 cm). Cut the hot pink vellum to approximately 4¼ x 9½ inches (10.8 x 24.1 cm).

4. Fold the bottom of the light pink vellum 3¼ inches (8.3 cm) up, using the bone folder for a sharp fold. Fold the top down 3 inches (7.6 cm), measuring from the longest point you cut the lace, to create the 4-inch (10.2 cm) tall envelope.

5. Fold the bottom of the hot pink vellum 3½ inches (8.9 cm) up, again using the bone folder for a sharp fold. Fold the top down 2 inches (5.1 cm), measuring from the longest point you cut the lace, to make the 4¼-inch (10.8 cm) square envelope.

6. Machine stitch the sides of the envelope ⅛ inch (3 mm) inside the edge. Use a large stitch and the matching thread.

7. To place each button, put a piece of clear tape cut to ¾ x ¾ inch (1.9 x 1.9 cm) on the inside of the flap under where the button will go. Using the matching thread and the hand sewing needle, double the thread and tie a knot at the end. Run the needle from the top side of the flap down through the flap and tape. The button will hide the knot. Run the needle back up to the top and stitch the button in place, running the thread through four times. Tie a knot under the button, and cut off the thread. Put another piece of tape over the first and the thread. This will secure the button.

8. To seal the envelopes once the invitations are inside, either use a glue stick or the envelope glue recipe provided on page 16.

Variations

You can vary the color of the paper you use as a background for the lace. Light and dark green are a good combination. If you can find a piece of colored lace (such as gold and pink), print it on the vellum with a white paper background for an elegant look.

Mary Lou
Holvenstot

Slide one
inside
the other,
forever!

to infinity

what you need

Finished Size

Largest envelope:
3 ¾ x 2 ¼ inches
(9.5 x 5.7 cm)
Smallest envelope:
⅝ x ⅜ inch
(1.6 x 1.0 cm)

what you do

1. Use a photocopier to create successively smaller copies of the template. The sizes shown were each reduced by 80 percent.

2. Cut out and place each template on the unprinted side of the patterned paper. Trace around each template with a pencil.

3. Carefully cut out the envelope shapes, cutting just inside the pencil lines so they don't show after assembly.

4. Place one of the envelope shapes unprinted side up on your work surface. Fold the two smaller flaps toward the center.

5. Fold the two larger flaps toward the center.

6. If desired, use a bone folder to sharpen the folds.

7. Unfold the two larger flaps. Apply glue to the edges of the bottom flap where it overlaps the smaller flaps.

8. Refold the bottom flap into place, pressing firmly until the glue takes hold.

9. Repeat steps 4 through 8 for each of the different-sized envelope templates.

10. Create a tiny card, insert it into the smallest of the envelopes, and then tuck each envelope into the next larger one in the series. To close the largest envelope, either tuck the top flap underneath the bottom one or apply a decorative sticker to seal it.

Joan K. Morris

paper

exchange

Create vinyl pockets, vary the prints

what you need

Tool box (page 12)

Clear vinyl, thin to medium thickness, 9½ x 18 inches (24.1 x 45.7 cm)

Thread in the color of your choice

1 package of ¼-inch-wide (6 mm) double-fold bias tape, in a coordinating color (optional)

Masking tape

Sewing machine

Wax paper

Assorted 8½ x 11-inch (21.6 x 27.9 cm) patterned papers

3 covered hair elastics, in a coordinating color

Finished Size
9¼ x 3¾ inches
(23.5 x 9.5 cm)

what you do

1. If you wish to make a plain-edged envelope, skip to step 3. To make a colored bias-tape-edged envelope, begin by cutting two pieces of the bias tape, each 9½ inches (24.1 cm) long.

2. Machine stitch the bias tape in position along the 9½-inch (24.1 cm) edges of the piece of vinyl. Make sure to catch the top and bottom of the bias tape with the vinyl in between. The bias tape has one side of the fold that is longer than the other. It's best to place the longer side on the bottom and the short side on top. Be sure the vinyl is all the way into the fold.

3. Next, for both the plain-edged and bias-edged variations, fold both 9½-inch-long

(24.1 cm) edges of the piece of vinyl 3½ inches (8.9 cm) in and tape in place with the masking tape. If you're making the bias-edged envelope, skip to step 5. If you're making the plain-edged envelope, continue with step 4.

4. For the plain envelope only: Using a large-stitch setting on the sewing machine, stitch the edges of the folds in place ⅛ inch (3 mm) in from the edge. Sometimes the vinyl will catch on the sewing machine foot. If this happens, place a small sheet of wax paper between the foot and the vinyl, lining the edge of the wax paper up with the edge of the vinyl, and stitch through the wax paper. When you are finished sewing, pull the wax paper off. If any of the wax

paper stays in the seams, lightly scrape it off with your nails. Skip to step 8.

5. Cut two pieces of the bias tape, each 11½ inches (29.2 cm) long. These are stitched to the 11-inch (27.9 cm) sides created when you folded the ends in.

6. To start the tape with a clean edge, open the folds of one end of the tape, fold it in ¼ inch (6 mm), then fold the tape back the way it was. Start with this folded end at one of the 11-inch (27.9 cm) ends and stitch into position.

7. Three inches (7.6 cm) before the other end, stop the sewing machine with the needle down. Open the end of the tape, fold ¼ inch (6 mm) in, and refold the tape to create the finished end. Stitch to the end.

8. With the sewn piece of vinyl open, slide the patterned paper, plain side up, into the pocket you've created. Then fold the envelope in thirds and place the covered elastics around the envelope to hold it in position.

Variation
Use two different colors of bias tape, one for the 11-inch (27.9 cm) sides and one for the 9½-inch (24.1 cm) sides.

perfect
score

Prop pictures on chevron stands

Christine Meissner

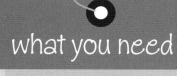

what you need

Tool Box (page 12)

Card stock, 6½ x 11 inches
(16.5 x 27.9 cm)

Photocopy of single and double
chevron templates, page 122

Photograph, 4 x 6 inches
(10.2 x 15.2 cm)

Double-sided tape or glue stick

Finished Size
4½ x 6½ inches
(11.4 x 16.5 cm)

what you do

1. Using the ruler and pencil, mark the 11-inch (27.9 cm) sides of the card stock at 4 inches (10.2 cm) and 8½ inches (21.6 cm). Use the bone folder to score a straight line and fold the paper into three sections.

2. Measure 1 inch (2.5 cm) in from the edge of the 4-inch (10.2 cm) section of the card. Using the ruler and pencil, trace a single chevron pattern, about ⅜ inch (1 cm) thick, centered on the card. The chevron should be about 2¼ inches (5.7 cm) long.

3. Cut out the long edges of the design using sharp scissors or a craft knife, then score on the short edges. Fold it back (see project photo).

4. Repeat steps 2 and 3 to draw and cut out the double chevron pattern on the 2½-inch (6.4 cm) section of card stock, with the following changes: Measure only ¼ inch (6 mm) from the edge of the card and make each chevron pattern only 2 inches (5.1 cm) long.

5. Attach the photo with tape or glue stick to the middle section. Tack the single chevron down with tape or glue if desired.

the big
easel

Frame a photo with card stock and yarn

Heather Isaacs

what you need

Tool Box (page 12)

Thin cardboard square, 8¼ x 8¼ inches (21 x 21 cm)

Craft knife with sharp blade

Card stock with two patterned sides, 12 x 12 inches
(30.5 x 30.5 cm)

Mat board in a complementary color to one side of the
card stock

Glue stick

Rubber stamps and ink pads (optional)

Hole punch, ⅛ inch (3 mm)

Decorative fibers or yarn

Finished Size
8¼ x 8¼ inches
(21 x 21 cm)

Variation
Use themed card stocks to coordinate the envelope and photo inside for special occasions, such as weddings, birthdays, holidays, or vacation memories.

what you do

1. Decide which side of the card stock will be the envelope exterior. The side facing up will become the interior of the envelope, which folds back into the easel. Using the thin cardboard square as a folding template, center it on the card stock so that the card stock forms four points under the template. The space between the edges of the template and the card stock allows the points to cover one another so that you can fasten the envelope shut. Fold each point down toward the center of the template.

2. Cut a piece of mat board to 5⅜ x 6⅞ inches (13.7 x 17.5 cm). Measure in 1 inch (2.5 cm) all around for a center opening of 3⅜ x 4⅞ inches (8.6 x 12.4 cm), to display a 3½ x 5-inch (8.9 x 12.7 cm) photo. Carefully cut out the opening. (If you have a mat cutting tool you can use it to make nice beveled edges.)

3. Center and glue the mat onto the interior side of the envelope. Glue three sides only so that a photo or piece of artwork can be slipped behind the mat. To make it easier to remove a photo, you can glue a tiny tab onto the back of the photo. The mat and background could be embellished at this time with rubber stamps or lightweight decorations.

4. Use the hole punch to make a hole in each of the four points of the envelope, about ½ inch (1.3 cm) from the tips. Cut a 12-inch (30.5 cm) length of fiber or yarn that can be laced through the four points to fasten the envelope. Feed through two holes so that the yarn goes under the points and can be brought back out the other two points to tie into a bow.

5. To use the envelope as an easel, untie the lacing and carefully fold each point backward. The easel will lean back on its own. The lacing could be used to loosely tie the four points together in the back to give more stability to the easel.

map it

Discover new directions for vintage paper

Lisa Presley

Tool Box (page 12)

Vintage atlas page, at least 5 x 11 inches (12.7 x 27.9 cm)

Multipurpose spray adhesive

Small scrap of pattern tissue

Vintage images, printed digital images, or purchased collage sheets

Vintage stamps

Small vintage button

Glue gun or quick-drying glue

1 strand of raffia, 8 inches (20.3 cm) long

2 pieces of clear vinyl, medium weight (6 to 8 gauge), each 7 x 12 inches (17.8 x 30.5 cm)

Pastry roller or rolling pin

Sewing machine

$7/16$-inch (1.1 cm) snap

Finished Size
4$\frac{1}{2}$ x 3$\frac{1}{2}$ inches
(11.4 x 8.9 cm)

what you do

1. Cut the main body of the gift card envelope from vintage atlas paper to form a 5 x 10-inch (12.7 x 25.4 cm) rectangle. Angle the corners of one short end of the rectangle to create an envelope "flap" shape.

2. Select the preferred side of the atlas page and lay it face up in front of you with the clipped corner ends facing down.

3. Focus your collage design on the lower 2$\frac{1}{2}$ inches (6.4 cm) of the atlas paper, centering the collage between the clipped corners.

4. Using spray adhesive, lightly spray the back of the pattern tissue and adhere it to the bottom left section of the area to be collaged.

5. Spray the collage images with adhesive and press into place on top of the pattern tissue.

6. Using the glue gun, glue the button into place.

7. Lay a piece of raffia across the face of the collaged section, loop or swirl the raffia slightly, and in two or three places glue it down with a very small dot of glue from the glue gun.

8. Lay one of the vinyl pieces on a flat surface. Using the spray adhesive, very lightly spray the side of the atlas paper that has the collage. Center the sprayed paper on top of the piece of vinyl, glue side down. Use a pastry roller or rolling pin to press the paper and vinyl together, rolling out any bubbles.

9. Lightly spray one side of the second piece of vinyl. Center it over the top of the completed paper and vinyl piece, glue side down, creating a sandwich. Roll out again to remove any bubbles.

10. Trim around the entire paper to remove any extra vinyl.

11. On the sewing machine, sew the end of the piece opposite the collage design with a straight-line stitch, approximately ¼ inch (6 mm) from the edge.

12. Fold the sewn edge of paper and vinyl up approximately 3½ inches (8.9 cm) to create an envelope pocket. Make sure that the collaged design area is in the proper position. If you are looking at the envelope pocket, the collage design should be on the back.

13. Sew around the envelope with a straight seam, ¼ inch (6 mm) from the edge. Start at the bottom left side and sew up one side, around the collaged portion, and back down to the bottom right side. Do not sew across the bottom edge.

14. Apply the top part of the snap first on the front of the envelope flap, according to the manufacturer's instructions, being sure to center it properly. Making sure that the top and bottom snap parts match up, position the lower section of the snap and apply.

Tips

A nonstick presser foot works best for sewing vinyl. If one is not available, a piece of gift-wrapping tissue paper can be laid over the area to be sewn to keep the presser foot from sticking to the vinyl. After sewing, gently tear away the tissue paper.

Most sewing machine tensions will need to be set high for sewing vinyl. Adjust the tension and practice on a piece of double-thickness vinyl before beginning to sew your project.

A very light spray of adhesive is all that is necessary to attach paper and vinyl. Too much spray will cloud the look of the images and paper.

Ready,
set, fold!

If it can be folded,
it should be folded—
with quick skill, undeniable style,
and a special message inside.

hush
hush

Conceal your message in confidential postcards

Lila Ruby King

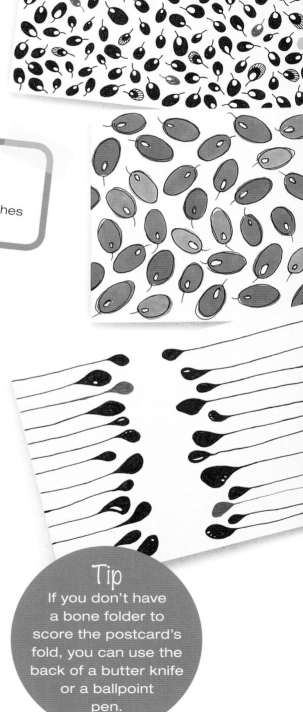

what you need

Tool Box (page 12)

Card stock or watercolor paper,
    any color

Steel ruler

Markers, pens, and pencils for
    decorating

Double-sided tape, preferably the
    type with a paper backing

Finished Size
Folded: 6 x 4 inches
(15.2 x 10.2 cm)
Unfolded: 8⅞ x 4 inches
(22.5 x 10.2 cm)

what you do

1. On the sheet of card stock or watercolor paper, measure a rectangle 8⅞ x 4 inches (22.5 x 10.2 cm) and cut it out with the craft knife. With your pencil, mark an extra line 3 inches (7.6 cm) in from one of the shorter sides.

2. Turn the card over and create your image or decoration, keeping in mind that you'll fold the card at the line you just drew—and it will be visible on the other side of the card once you are finished.

3. Turn the card back over and score along the pencil line. To do this, line up the ruler with the pencil line and run the bone folder along the line until a groove is formed. Erase the pencil line. You can now fold that segment over and press down along the crease to get it to sit nice and flat.

4. The right-hand section of the card that is left uncovered is where you will draw the lines for the address. You can neatly rule the lines, or do something more creative. If you like, you can also draw a box to show where the stamp will go.

5. Cut a strip of double-sided tape that is 3⅞ x ⁵⁄₁₆ inch (9.8 x 0.8 cm). Stick it down along the left-hand edge of the card, in the section that will be folded down. If you are not using the card immediately, it is best to use the double-sided tape that comes with a paper backing.

6. Once you have written your message, peel the paper backing from the tape, fold the card over, and press it down to stick.

Tip
If you don't have a bone folder to score the postcard's fold, you can use the back of a butter knife or a ballpoint pen.

Crease whiz

Master an ingenious fold

Elsje
van der Ploeg

Finished Size
5¾ x 3½ inches
(14.6 x 8.9 cm)

what you do

1. Turn the paper white side up. Make two helping folds, as follows: Fold the lower left-hand corner over to the right-hand side and unfold; then fold the lower right-hand corner over to the left-hand side and unfold. The folds you've made should look like an X, which runs from the bottom two corners up to the opposite sides.

2. Turn the paper over. Make another helping fold, this one horizontal, by folding the paper up so the fold crosses the middle of the X you made in step 1. Unfold and turn the paper back over to the white side.

3. Collapse along the fold lines by bringing the two ends of the horizontal helping fold together in the middle and flattening the triangle shape that is formed. You should now have a two-layered triangle shape on the bottom, with a rectangular shape at the top (figure 1).

4. Fold the upper layers of the triangle down to meet the triangle's point at the bottom. This fold creates a small square shape with corners at the top and bottom and a vertical slit in the middle.

5. Open the slit and push the bottom corner of the square up to meet the top corner (figure 2). This fold forms two smaller squares side by side.

6. Fold the top inside corners of the two squares down (figure 3). Fold the top point in the middle down as well.

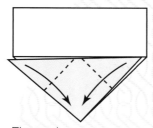

Figure 1

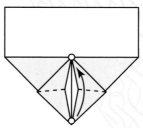

Figure 2

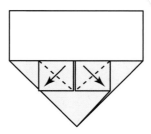

Figure 3

7. Fold the triangle located at the bottom up and over the smaller squares you were just working with. Fold the point of this triangle over the small center triangle and back behind it (figure 4). Smooth the folds.

8. Fold in the two sides of the paper the width of the rectangle you created in step 7. The paper should now measure about 5¾ x 7 inches (14.6 x 17.8 cm).

9. Fold in the top corners of the paper (figure 5). Bring the top point under the bottom fold to finish your envelope.

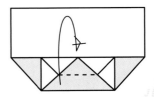

Figure 4

Figure 5

very fishy

Assemble an origami ocean

LOVE FROM : ELSJE VAN DER PLOEG - HOLLAND

MY FRIEND
HIS ADDRESS
COUNTRY

Elsje
van der Ploeg

what you need

Tool box (page 12)

Any A4-sized paper, approximately
  8¼ x 11¾ inches (21.0 x 29.8 cm),
  or a standard 8½ x 11-inch
  (21.6 x 27.9 cm) sheet also works

Decorative additions, such as ribbon,
  stickers, and buttons (optional)

Self-stick address label

what you do

1. Turn the paper white side up. Make two helping folds, as follows: Fold the upper left-hand corner over to the right-hand side and unfold; then fold the upper right-hand corner over to the left-hand side and unfold. The folds you've made should look like an X, which runs from the top two corners down to the opposite sides, about 2½ inches (6.4 cm) from the bottom of the paper.

2. Turn the paper over. Make another helping fold, this one horizontal, by folding the paper down 4¼ inches (10.8 cm) from the top, to a point 2½ inches (6.4 cm) from the bottom. This fold should intersect the X you formed in step 1. Unfold and turn the paper back over.

3. Collapse along the fold lines by bringing the two ends of the horizontal helping fold together in the middle and flattening the triangle shape that is formed. You should now have a two-layered triangle shape on top, with a rectangular shape underneath measuring 8½ x 2½ inches (21.6 x 6.4 cm). See figure 1.

Figure 1

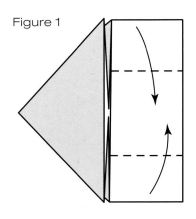

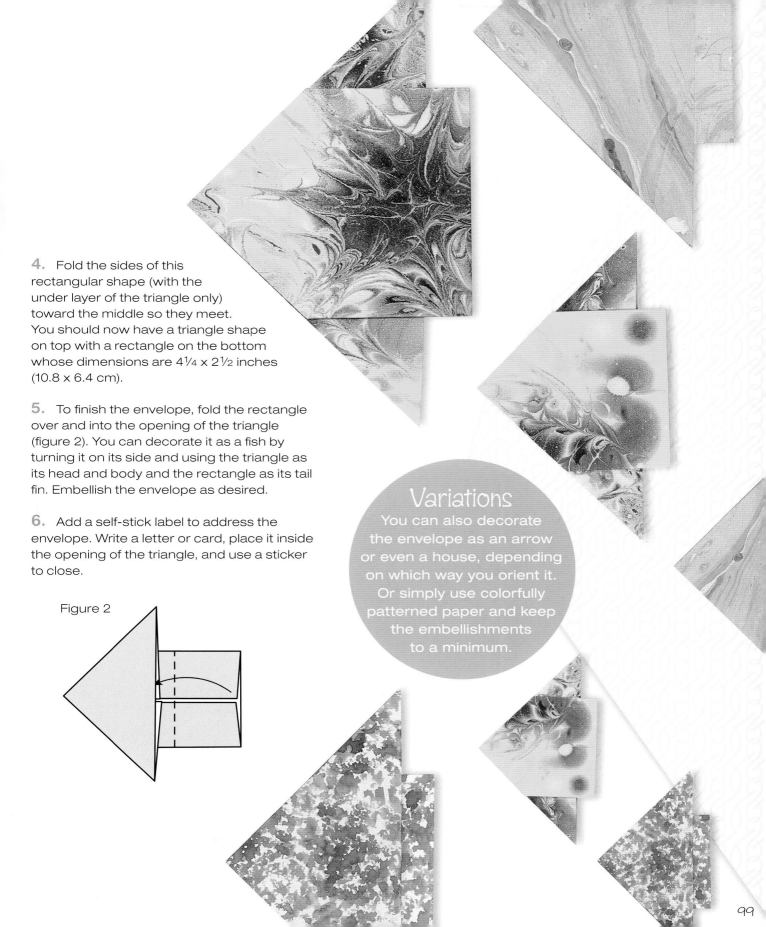

4. Fold the sides of this rectangular shape (with the under layer of the triangle only) toward the middle so they meet. You should now have a triangle shape on top with a rectangle on the bottom whose dimensions are 4¼ x 2½ inches (10.8 x 6.4 cm).

5. To finish the envelope, fold the rectangle over and into the opening of the triangle (figure 2). You can decorate it as a fish by turning it on its side and using the triangle as its head and body and the rectangle as its tail fin. Embellish the envelope as desired.

6. Add a self-stick label to address the envelope. Write a letter or card, place it inside the opening of the triangle, and use a sticker to close.

Figure 2

Variations

You can also decorate the envelope as an arrow or even a house, depending on which way you orient it. Or simply use colorfully patterned paper and keep the embellishments to a minimum.

placemat
bandit

Upgrade
quirky
pinched
paper

Elsje
van der Ploeg

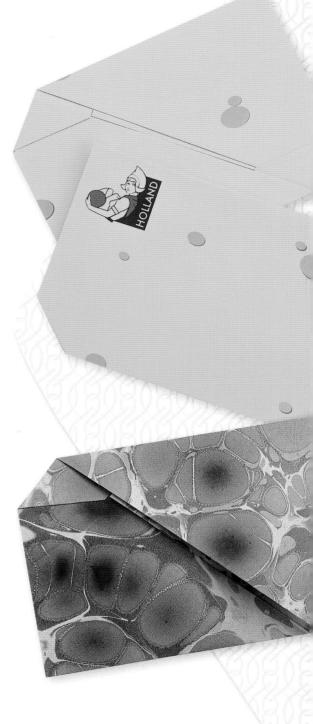

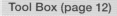

what you need

Tool Box (page 12)

Any A4-sized paper, such as gift wrap, newspaper,
stationery, or scrapbooking paper approximately
$8\frac{1}{4}$ x $11\frac{3}{4}$ inches (21.0 x 29.8 cm), a standard
$8\frac{1}{2}$ x 11-inch (21.6 x 27.9 cm) sheet also works

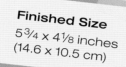

Finished Size
$5\frac{3}{4}$ x $4\frac{1}{8}$ inches
(14.6 x 10.5 cm)

what you do

1. Turn the paper white side up. Make a helping fold by folding the paper in half horizontally. Open the paper to expose the horizontal fold going across the middle.

2. Fold the top right-hand corner down to meet the fold. Then fold the bottom left-hand corner up to meet the fold.

3. Fold the top left edge in half, toward the upper triangle, so the edges meet. Then fold the bottom right edge in half, toward the lower triangle, so the edges meet (figure 1).

4. Fold the top left-hand corner down and under the folded right-hand edge. Fold the bottom right-hand corner up and under the folded left-hand edge (figure 2). Turn the envelope so it's aligned horizontally. And you're done!

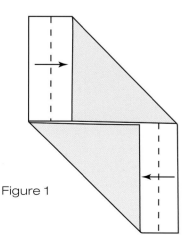

Figure 1

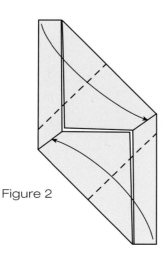

Figure 2

Christine Meissner

artful image

Paint outside, write inside

what you need

Tool Box (page 12)

High-density polyethylene
   envelope material

Wax paper

Sponge

Acrylic paints: one light color,
   one dark

Postage stamp

Finished Size
4⅛ x 5⅝ inches
(10.5 x 14.3 cm)

what you do

1. Measure and cut the envelope material with a craft knife to 8 x 11¼ inches (20.3 x 28.6 cm).

2. Place the envelope material on wax paper. After moistening the sponge with water, apply the light color acrylic paint to the front side of the material; then apply the dark color as desired, leaving areas of light color to show through. Repeat on the reverse side. Let dry.

3. Orient the sheet so the 8-inch (20.3 cm) sides are at the top and bottom. Fold the lower left-hand corner to approximately ½ inch (1.3 cm) from the right side of the paper.

4. Fold the upper right-hand corner so that the right edge of the corner touches the top edge of the previous fold.

5. Turn the sheet around so what was the upper left-hand corner is now a point at the bottom. Fold the bottom up so it lines up just below the triangle on the left side.

6. Fold the top down so the crease lines up with the point of the previous fold.

7. Fold the top point over to the front. The stamp will hold this tab down.

8. Unfold the mailer, write your letter, refold, and secure with the stamp.

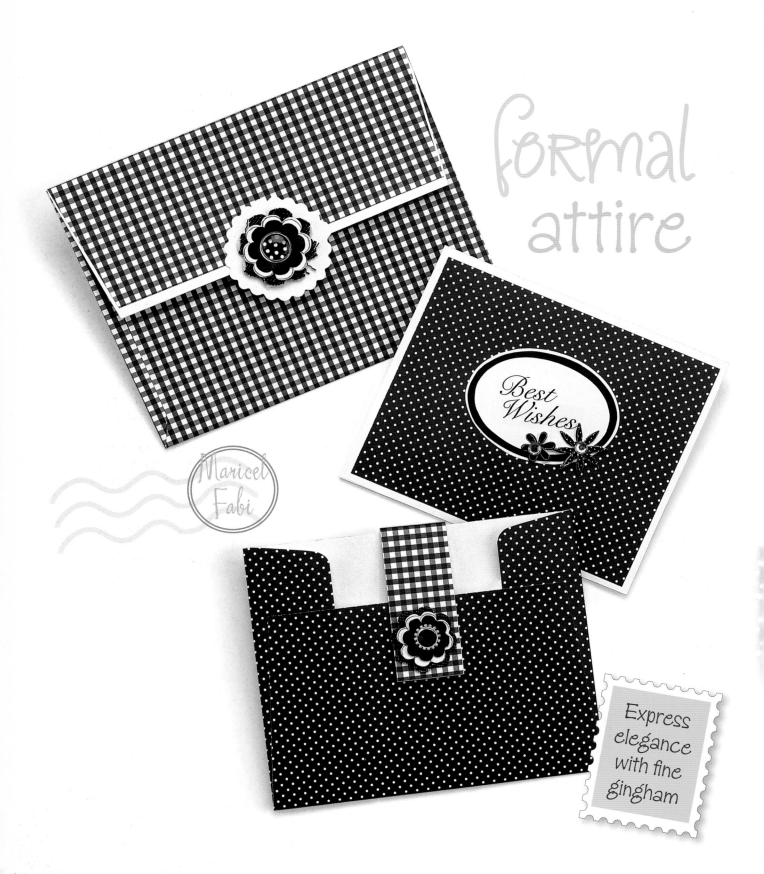

formal
attire

*Best
Wishes*

*Maricel
Fabi*

Express
elegance
with fine
gingham

what you need

Tool Box (page 12)

Templates (pages 123–124)

Dotted and gingham printed papers, each 12 x 12 inches (30.5 cm x 30.5 cm)

Double-sided tape

2 black flower stickers

White card stock

Decorative-edge scissors

Finished Size

Inner envelope: 5 x 4 inches (12.7 x 10.2 cm)

Outer envelope: 5³/₄ x 4¹/₂ inches (14.6 x 11.4 cm)

what you do

1. Trace the inner envelope template (page 123) onto the white side of the dotted paper. Cut it out with the craft knife and ruler. Fold along the template's dotted lines using the bone folder. Apply the tape on the edges of the bottom flap, turn this up, and stick it to the side flaps.

2. Using the tab closure template (page 123), cut out the shape from the gingham-printed paper. Attach it vertically to the back side of the envelope. Turn the envelope over and fold down the top edge of the tab closure. Adhere a flower sticker at the end.

3. Trace the outer envelope template (page 124) onto the gingham-printed paper and cut it out. Fold along the template's dotted lines using the bone folder. Apply the tape on the edges of the bottom flap, turn this up, and stick it to the side flaps.

4. Next, trace the top flap onto the white card stock. Cut it slightly larger than the top flap to create a white edge. Apply tape to attach it.

5. Draw a circle or trace a round object onto white card stock and trim with the decorative-edge scissors. Attach it to the top flap, and stick the flower on as a final touch.

Tip
To make the envelope reclosable, glue matching pieces of hook-and-loop tape to the flap and envelope.

be mine

Indulge your cherished Valentine

Elsje van der Ploeg

Finished Size

4⅛ x 4¾ inches
(10.5 x 12.1 cm)

what you do

1. Turn the paper white side up. Fold in half horizontally; open the paper. Fold in half vertically; open the paper. Next, make two helping folds by folding the long edges to the middle. Open the paper to expose the eight folded sections.

2. Turn the paper over. Fold the bottom left and right corners up to meet the helping fold lines you've made.

3. Fold up the bottom (figure 1). The fold should be approximately 2¼ inches (5.7 cm) from the bottom of the paper—or 1½ inches (3.8 cm) if using the smaller size paper (see Variation at right).

4. Turn the paper back over to the white side. Fold the top left and right corners down to meet the helping fold lines. Fold both long edges to the middle (figure 2).

5. Make a helping fold by folding the top left and right corners down; then unfold.

6. Form the shape of a heart (with two points at the top): With your finger, open up the top left and right triangles by pulling them toward you and flattening. You should have made two small triangle shapes pointing down. Fold them up again and flatten so the points are facing up (figure 3).

7. Fold down the top triangle toward the back and turn the paper over. You've formed a heart shape! Now fold up the bottom of the piece at the horizontal fold line you made earlier, so that its top edge goes under the heart shape (figure 4).

Variation

You can create a mini heart envelope by starting with a smaller piece of paper. Try a sheet in the European A5 size, approximately 5¾ x 8¼ inches (14.6 x 21 cm).

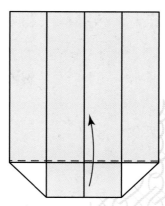

Figure 1

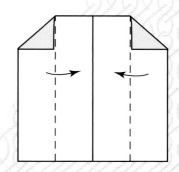

Figure 2

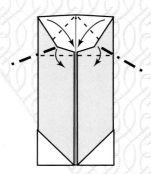

Figure 3

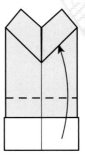

Figure 4

pop-up culture

Design stationery that hinges on perfection

Let success be measured by the happiness in your heart.

do your best.

Melony Bradley

what you need

Tool Box (page 12)

Template (page 125)

Double-sided patterned papers

Paper trimmer with scoring blade

Super sticky tape, 1/4 inch (6 mm)

Coordinating scraps of card stock

Rubber stamp

Pigment ink

Various-sized hole punches

Acrylic rhinestones

Paper adhesive or glue stick

Self-stick pop-up hinges

Finished Size
4 x 5⅞ inches
(10.2 x 14.9 cm)

what you do

1. Using the template, trace on one side of the patterned paper. Cut it out.

2. Use the paper trimmer to score the top flap 3 inches (7.6 cm) from the flap's point. Score the bottom flap 3¼ inches (8.3 cm) from the bottom. Use sticky tape to adhere only the left and right edges together.

3. To make the pop-up card, trim a 2½-inch (6.4 cm) square of coordinating card stock. Trim a 2-inch (5.1 cm) square from the remaining patterned paper scraps. Stamp the desired image on the paper square with pigment ink. Use a paper punch and rhinestones to embellish the stamped image. Attach the stamped paper to the card stock with paper adhesive or a glue stick.

4. To adhere the pop-up to the envelope, stick two hinges to the left and right edges of the square back, with the adhesive facing forward. Adhere the pop-up to the inside flap of the envelope by lining up the ends of the hinges with the score of the envelope, and centering it.

5. Embellish inside the envelope's top flap, back of flap, and bottom as desired.

templates

Sunny Flowers

page 32

Top Secret

page 34
Enlarge 200%

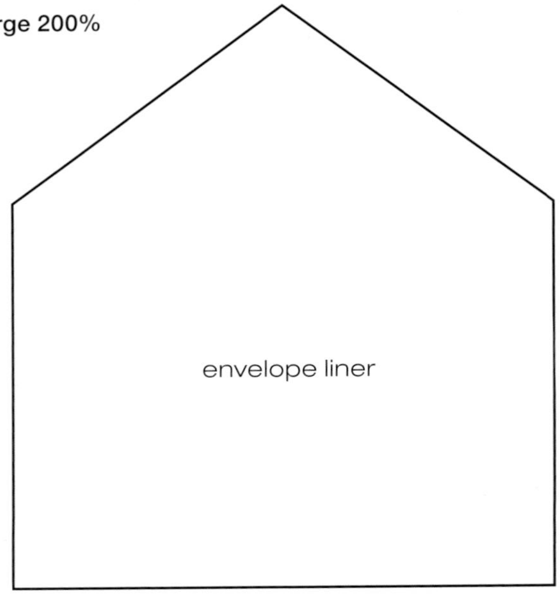

envelope liner

Top Secret

page 34
Enlarge 200%

top flap

fold

side
flap

fold

envelope

fold

side
flap

glue

fold

bottom flap

glue here

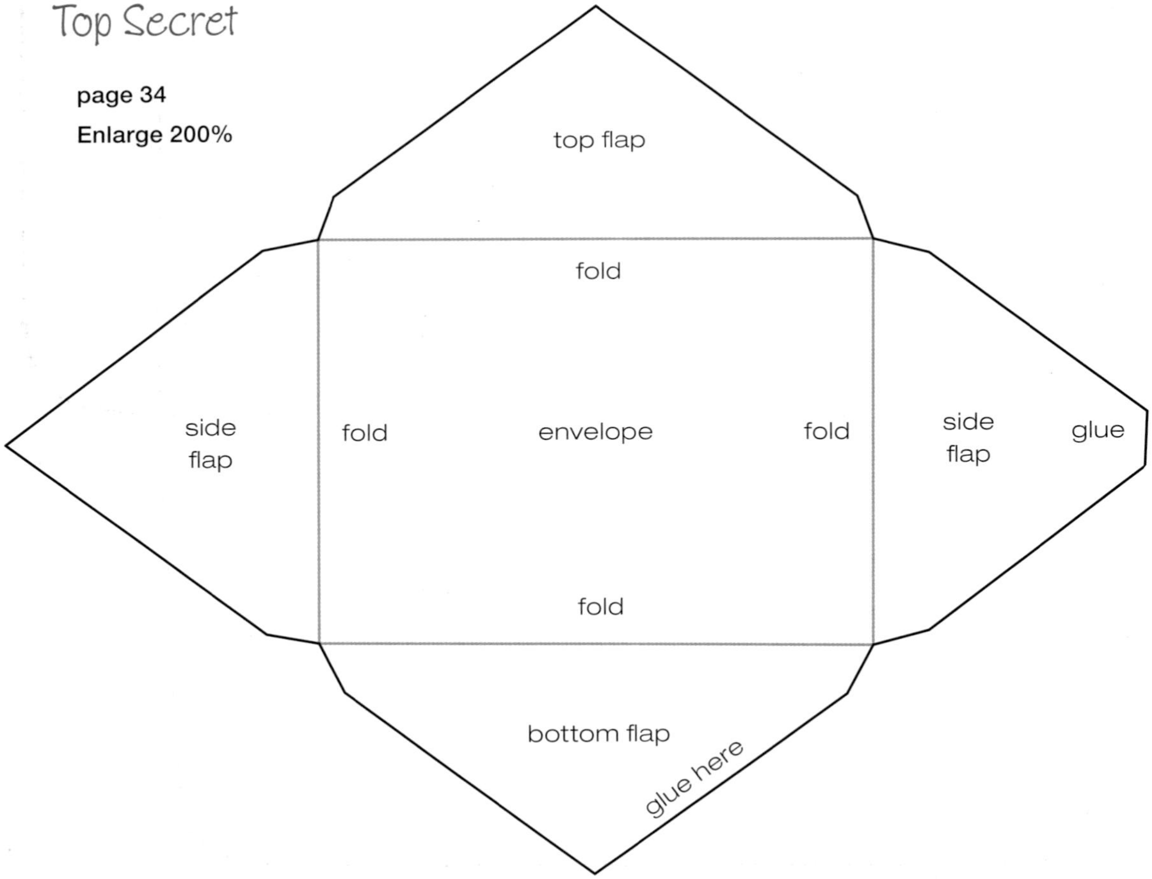

Smart Sack

page 40

Enlarge 145%

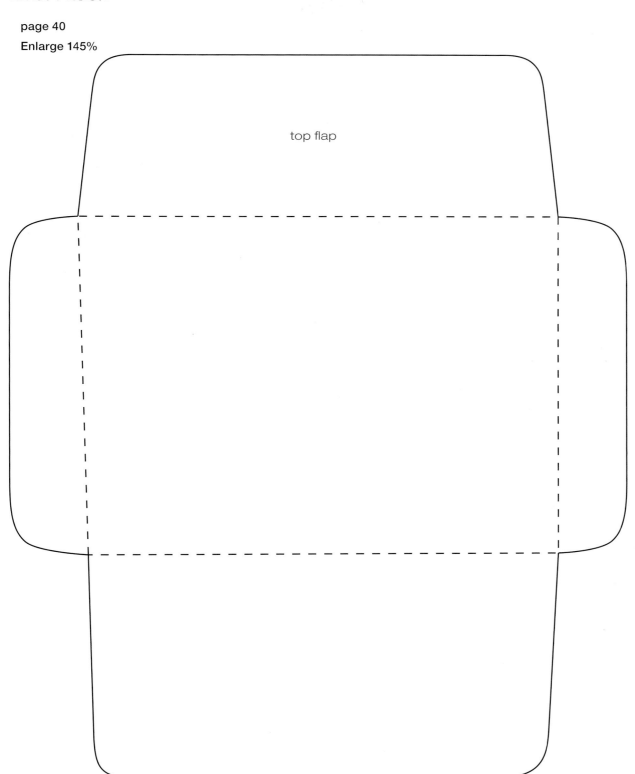

top flap

Patchwork Garden

page 45

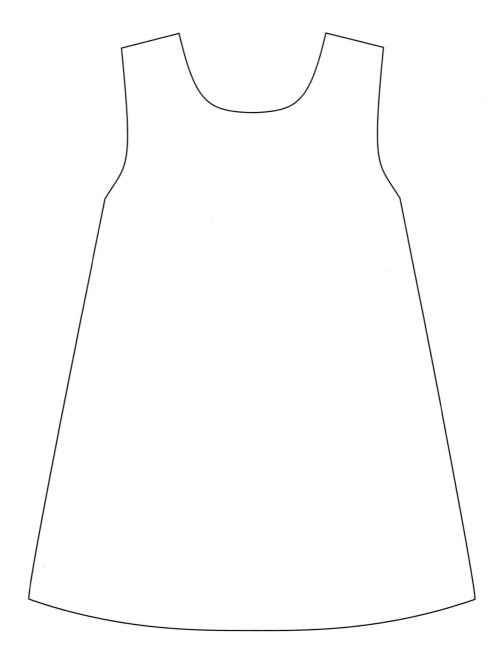

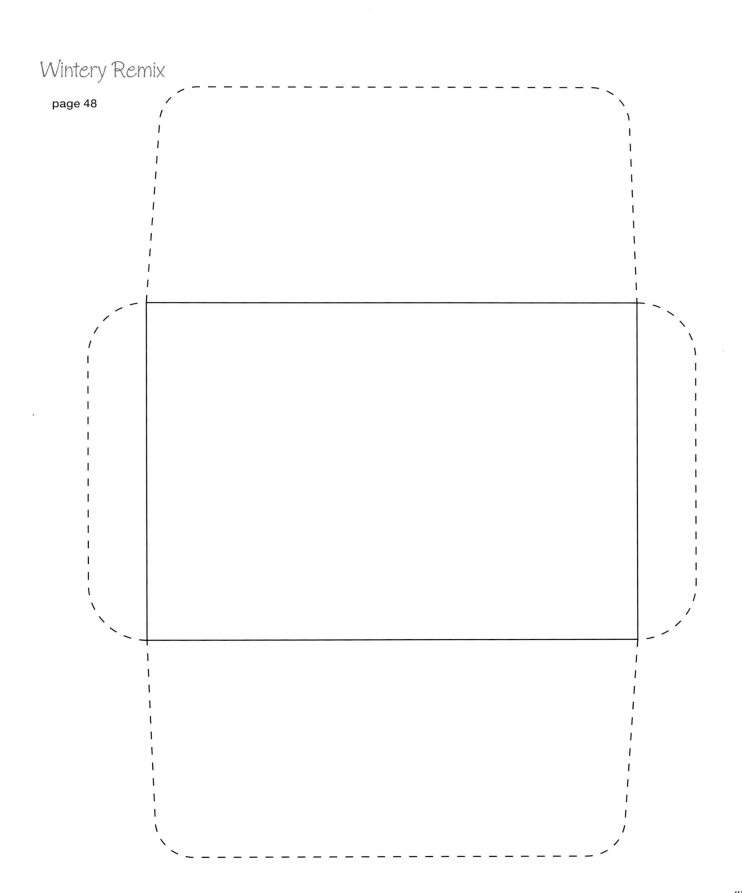

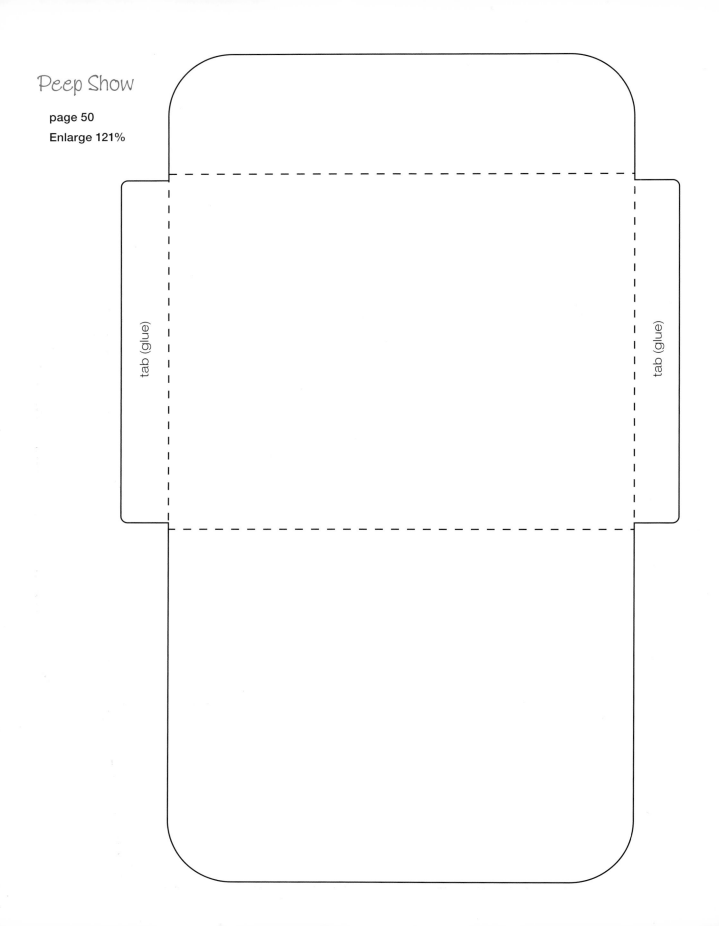

Peep Show

page 50
Enlarge 121%

tab (glue)

tab (glue)

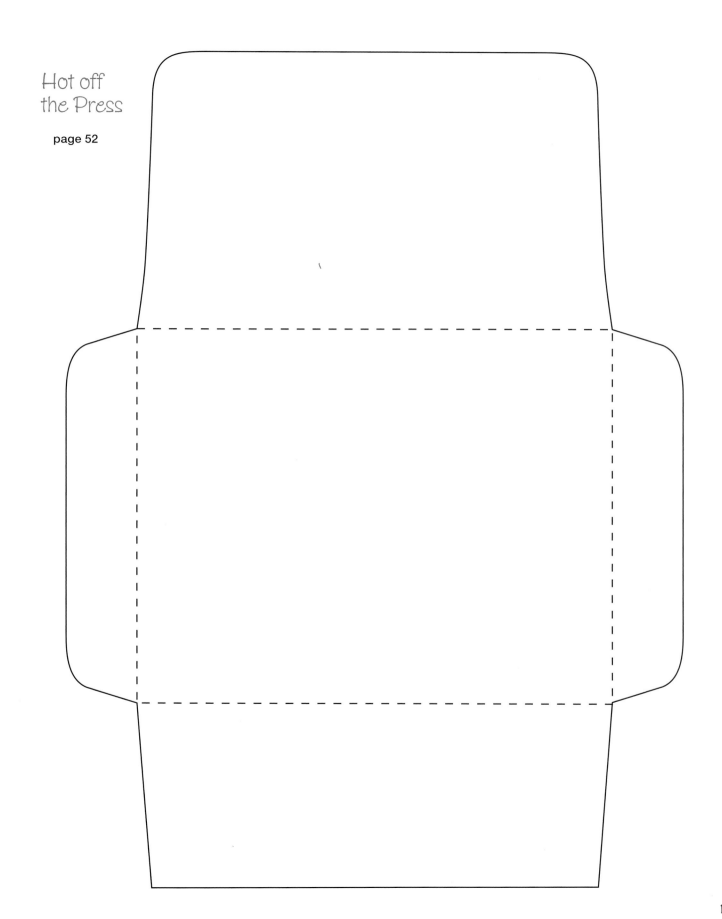

Hot off
the Press

page 52

Peel-n-Stick

The Catalog Envelope
page 54
Enlarge 250%

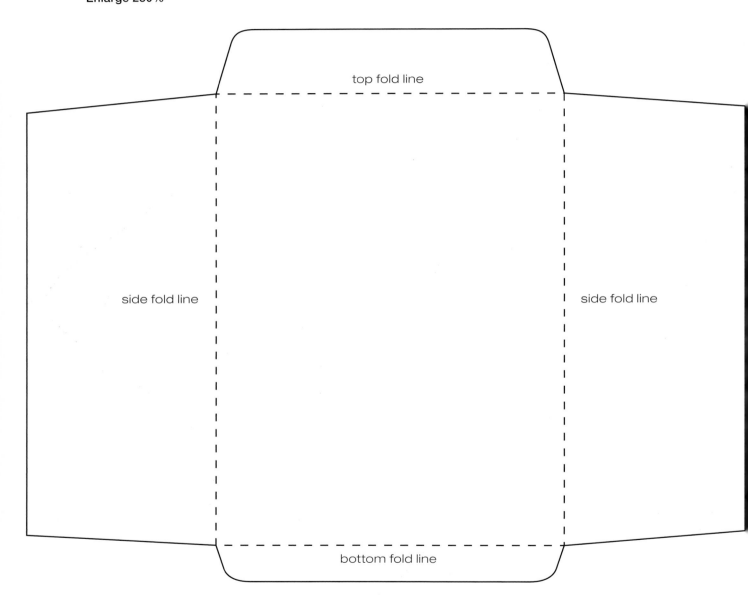

top fold line

side fold line

side fold line

bottom fold line

Peel-n-Stick

The CD Envelope
page 54
Enlarge 200%

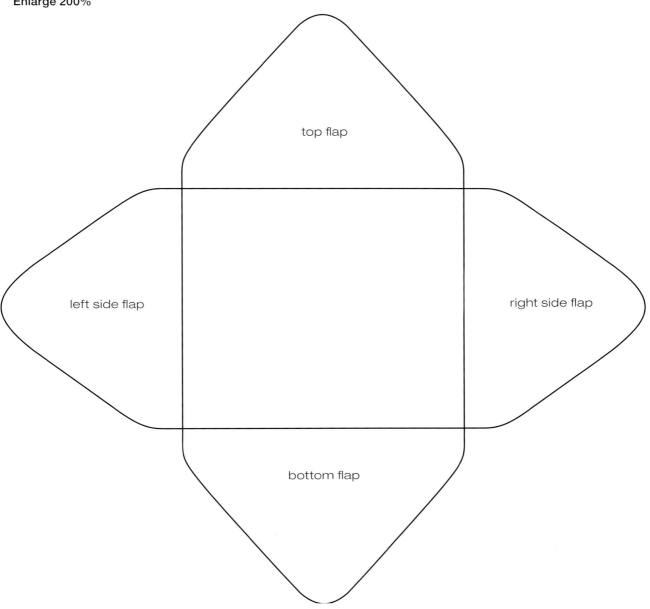

Small Enterprise

page 70

Teeny Tags

Envelope
page 72

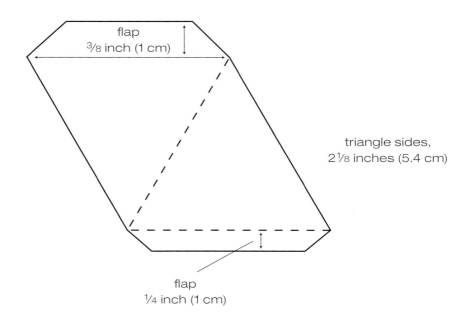

flap
⅜ inch (1 cm)

triangle sides,
2⅛ inches (5.4 cm)

flap
¼ inch (1 cm)

Teeny Tags

Card Insert
page 72

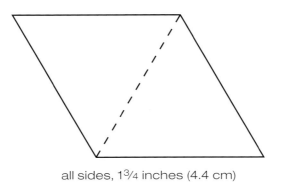

all sides, 1¾ inches (4.4 cm)

To Infinity

page 80

Reduce each copy
by 80% to make
smaller and smaller
envelopes.

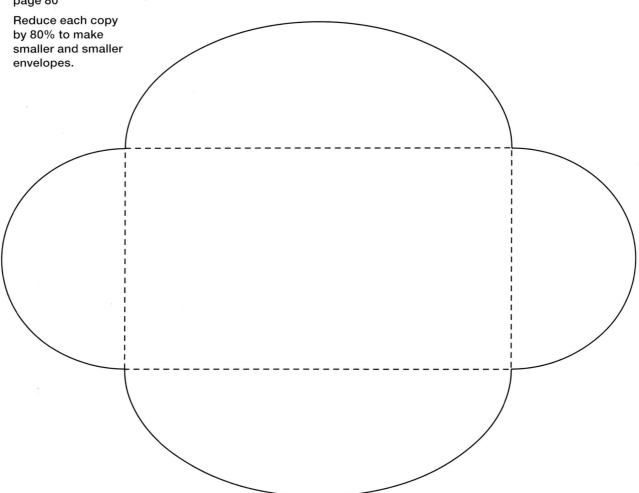

Perfect Score

page 84

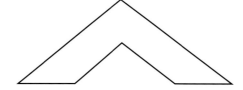

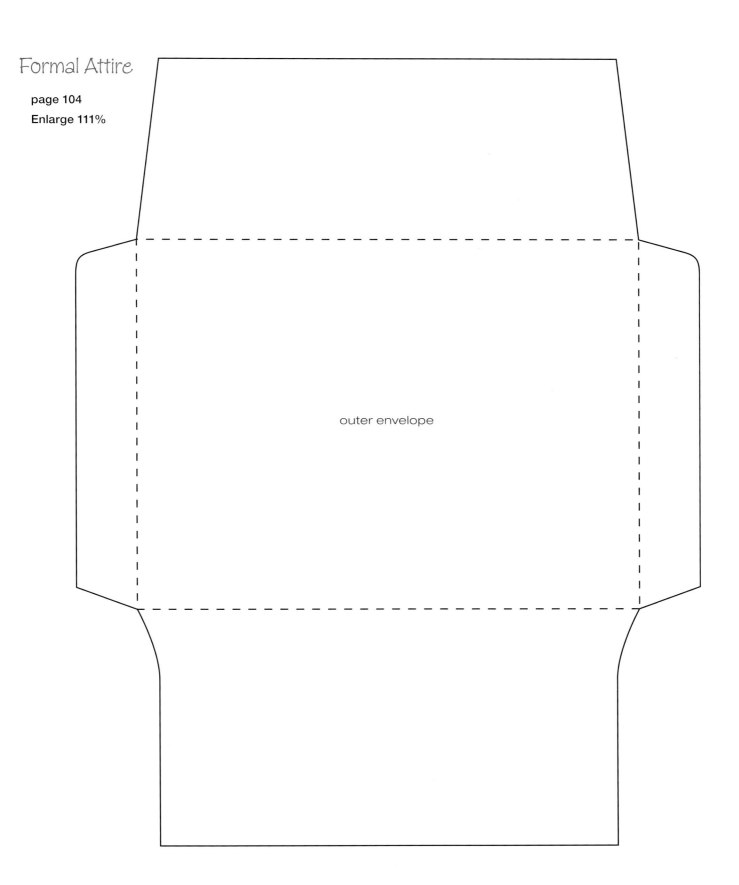

Formal Attire

page 104
Enlarge 111%

outer envelope

Formal Attire

page 104

Enlarge 111%

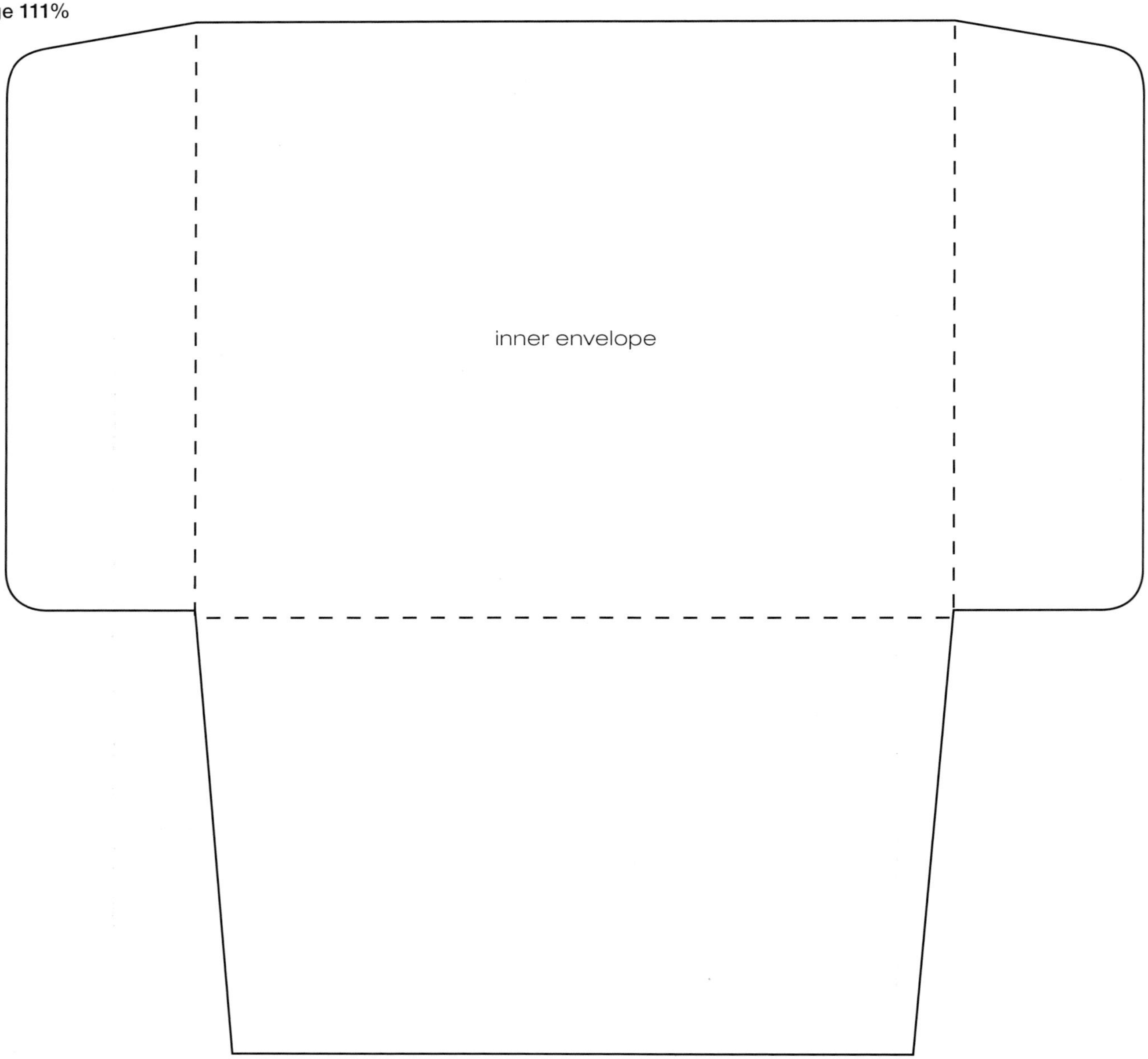

inner envelope

Formal Attire

page 104

Enlarge 111%

tab closure

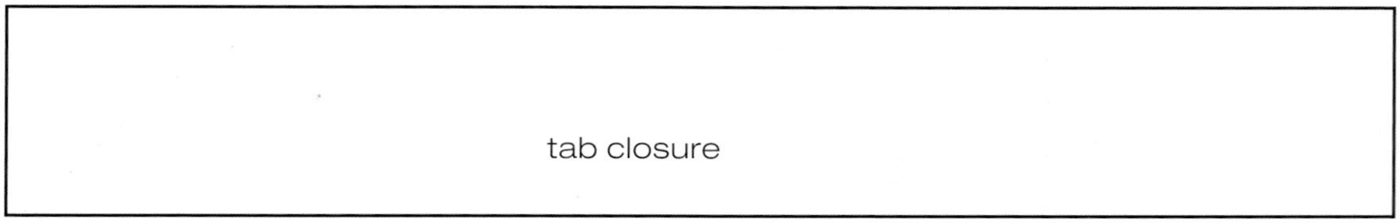

Pop-Up Culture

page 108

Enlarge 125%

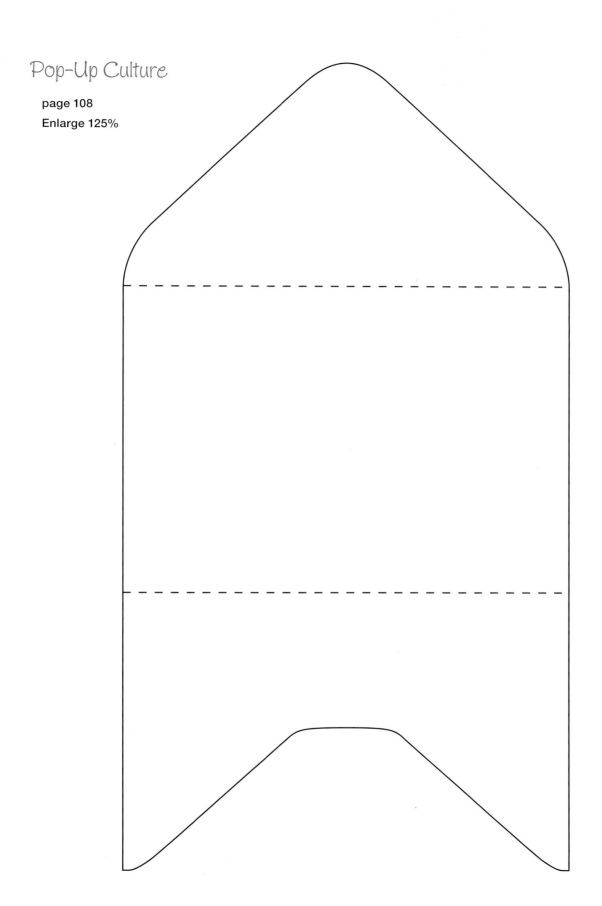

ABOUT THE DESIGNERS

Melony Bradley is a full-time creative designer specializing in beaded crafts, recycled crafts, and kids projects. When she's not working on project design, she writes technique articles for the craft industry. A member of the Craft & Hobby Association (CHA), Melony demonstrates at trade shows and teaches classes. She has been published in numerous magazines and has worked for several publishers.

Johanna Chambers is an artist and illustrator whose work has won numerous awards. Many of her jewelry pieces and works of art have been show-cased in galleries in Washington and California. Several of her paintings reside at the Catskill Animal Sanctuary in New York State. Johanna loves teaching art and hopes to illustrate children's books. See her work at www.johannachambers. deviantart.com.

Heather Crossley is a mixed media artist who delights in transforming discarded objects into artful and purposeful things. Her work has appeared in many U.S. and Australian magazines, including on the covers of at least five. She's contributed projects to books like *500 Handmade Books* and *Artful Paper Dolls* (both by Lark Books). See more of her work at www.powerup.com.au/~mkhc.

Maricel Fabi began her love affair with paper at an early age by collecting stationery. She started her art career making greeting cards for friends and family. Since then, she's broadened her range to other paper crafts like children's crafts, gift wrapping, and home decorating. A self-taught artist, she enjoys the challenge of developing new ideas and designs. View her work at www.maricelv.blogspot.com.

Mar Goman is a multi-media artist who has been exhibiting her work around the Northwest for thirty years. Her specialties include drawing and painting, fibers, collage, embroidery, sculpture, assemblage, and book arts. She uses a combination of found materials and traditional art supplies. Mar usually has more than a dozen different projects going at once. Check out her online gallery at sedersgallery.com.

Fiona Hesford sells her quirky freelance textile designs to fashion companies all over the world. Presently, she's developing a collection of handmade products for the home (available at www.girls-institute.co.uk). Her kitchen accessories include tea cozies, aprons, bags, cushions, and other vibrant, funky stuff. Her work has been featured in *Elle Decoration* and *Marie Claire* magazines, both in the UK.

Mary Hettmansperger is a fiber/jewelry artist who has exhibited and taught across the U.S. and abroad. She authored and illustrated *Fabulous Woven Jewelry* and *Wrap, Stitch, Fold & Rivet* (both by Lark Books). You can find her work in many magazines and on television programs such as *Beads Baubles and Jewels*. Find out more at www.maryhetts.com.

Jennie Hinchcliff is an active participant in the international mail art community. She teaches classes in mail art and faux postage throughout the West Coast, and she produces the quarterly mail art zine *Red Letter Day*. As one half of Pod Post, she encourages people to share their love for writing letters and sending art via the postal system. See for yourself at www.podpodpost.com.

Mary Lou Holvenstot has made arts and crafts a way of life. While climbing the corporate ladder, she kept her sanity by drawing, bead weaving, and cross-stitching. Now retired, she creates whimsical drawings for her Captioned Critters and Understated Greetings lines. She also designs bead-woven jewelry and art pieces. See more at www.time2cre8.com and time2cre8.etsy.com.

Heather Isaacs is an artisan and author whose how-to projects and profiles of fellow artists have been featured in *American Miniaturist, Dollhouse Miniatures*, and *Renaissance* magazines. She builds 1/12th scale models of real-life objects (such as buildings and the like) using wood, polymer clay, and paper.

Lila Ruby King is a designer and jewelry artist whose work is in numerous private collections all over the world. While avidly pursuing environmentally friendly techniques for both her jewelry and paper-based works, she has teamed up with artists from all over the world to share and develop green art and green living ideas. Go to www.lilarubyking.eu to see her jewelry and paper art.

Sarah Lightfoot-Brundage produces one-of-a-kind hand-knit and fulled Icelandic wool handbags, as well as hand-felted Merino wool scarves, wraps, and jewelry. A member of the New England Felt Makers Guild, she has had her work displayed in gallery exhibits, juried creative arts festivals, and fine boutiques. To see her work under the name Thistle Downs wool design, visit www.smashingdarling.com.

Christine Meissner is a mixed media artist who's not afraid to dabble. Her work has appeared in such diverse magazines as *Somerset Studio*, *Bead Unique*, and *Scripsit*, the journal of the Washington Calligraphers Guild. Her artwork has also been included in the collection of the Aurora Women's Health Center in Milwaukee, Wisconsin. Check out her Wit's End Studio blog at christinemeissner.blogspot.com.

Joan K. Morris's artistic endeavors have led her down many successful creative paths, from ceramics to costume design for motion pictures. She has contributed projects for numerous Lark Books publications, including *Extreme Office Crafts*, *Cutting-Edge Decoupage*, *Button! Button!*, *Pretty Little Presents*, *50 Nifty Beaded Cards*, and many more. Regardless of the craft, Joan is an innovative designer.

Elizabeth Nolin Pickett wears many hats, including interior designer and historic preservationist. She credits her mother for teaching her to love crafts. In high school, she sold handcrafted stationery and jewelry. Now she has her own shop, Bittersweet Design Studio, and has even helped her daughter with her shop, Moonshine Essentials. For more information, visit www.bittersweetdesignstudio.com.

Lisa Presley is a crafter who loves all things vintage—especially vintage papers and findings. She sells her collage and paper art in shops and boutiques in the Kansas City, Missouri, area, but you can browse her work and buy it for yourself (or your friends) at her online storefront at mypapergarden.etsy.com.

Sharon Rohloff has enjoyed experimenting with paper and paint all her life. Trained as a graphic artist, she started crafting as a rubber stamp artist. Now she teaches altered book art and card making. She enjoys combining sewing with paper arts and looks for opportunities to include vintage materials whenever possible. You can see more of Sharon's designs in *50 Nifty Beaded Cards* (by Lark Books).

Amy Jean Rowan is an artist, designer, and entrepreneur working under the moniker Art School Girl. She developed her first product in art school: a blank journal made from recycled books. Since then, she's collected and resuscitated many old, broken, library discards into greetings, books, bookmarks, and art that's sold across the U.S. and Canada. See her latest reclaimed projects at www.artschoolgirl.com.

Cathy Schellenberg is a creative scrapbooker and paper artist. Her work has been showcased in more than 30 different magazines and books in six different countries. She teaches card-making classes while designing for a variety of online and print scrapbooking and craft paper magazines. Somehow, she finds time to maintain a blog. Visit cathysartblog.blogspot.com to see more of her artwork.

Elsje van der Ploeg, a Dutch writer who founded the Envelope and Letter Folds Association, has created and diagrammed more than 300 mail models. She's also written more than 25 craft books about decorating paper, drawing, painting, origami, photos, rubberstamps, and mini-mandalas. She gives workshops throughout Europe.

About the Author

Marthe Le Van is a senior craft editor for Lark Books, where her creative spirit, enthusiasm for detail, and esteem for the human imagination can thrive. Since 2000, she has written, edited, juried, or curated more than 30 titles, including most recently *Stencil Me In* and *Stitched Jewels*. She's always had a sweet spot for creating special packaging and loves when a handcrafted envelope appears in her mailbox.

Acknowledgments

I'm fortunate to have received so many innovative envelope projects from our 20 contributing crafters. Your imagination and talent never ceases to amaze me. Special thanks for sending so many variations of your work—the added effort really helped brighten every page.

The Lark Books team that developed and designed *Pushing the Envelope* is extremely hard working and gifted. Larry Shea, Mark Bloom, and Gavin Young provided consistent editorial support. Art contributors Celia Naranjo, Dana Irwin, and Kay Stafford offered fresh, inventive ideas with stellar results. Photographer Stewart O'Shields, illustrator Orrin Lundgren, and cover designer Lana Lee shared their superb artistry, and I am so grateful for their exceptional abilities.

Finally, thanks to our enthusiastic readers for your continued passion for all things crafty. You give us the inspiration to make every publication our absolute best.

Index

Index of Artists